USING MICROSOFT EXCEL FOR SOCIAL RESEARCH

Sara Miller McCune founded SAGE Publishing in 1965 to support the dissemination of usable knowledge and educate a global community. SAGE publishes more than 1000 journals and over 800 new books each year, spanning a wide range of subject areas. Our growing selection of library products includes archives, data, case studies and video. SAGE remains majority owned by our founder and after her lifetime will become owned by a charitable trust that secures the company's continued independence.

Los Angeles | London | New Delhi | Singapore | Washington DC | Melbourne

USING MICROSOFT EXCEL FOR SOCIAL RESEARCH

CHARLOTTE BROOKFIELD

Los Angeles | London | New Delhi
Singapore | Washington DC | Melbourne

Los Angeles | London | New Delhi
Singapore | Washington DC | Melbourne

SAGE Publications Ltd
1 Oliver's Yard
55 City Road
London EC1Y 1SP

SAGE Publications Inc.
2455 Teller Road
Thousand Oaks, California 91320

SAGE Publications India Pvt Ltd
B 1/I 1 Mohan Cooperative Industrial Area
Mathura Road
New Delhi 110 044

SAGE Publications Asia-Pacific Pte Ltd
3 Church Street
#10-04 Samsung Hub
Singapore 049483

Editor: Jai Seaman
Assistant editor: Charlotte Bush
Assistant editor, digital: Sunita Patel
Production editor: Victoria Nicholas
Marketing manager: Susheel Gokarakonda
Cover design: Shaun Mercier
Typeset by: C&M Digitals (P) Ltd, Chennai, India
Printed in the UK

Library of Congress Control Number: 2020940588

British Library Cataloguing in Publication data

A catalogue record for this book is available from the British Library

ISBN 978-1-5264-6834-5
ISBN 978-1-5264-6833-8 (pbk)

At SAGE we take sustainability seriously. Most of our products are printed in the UK using responsibly sourced papers and boards. When we print overseas we ensure sustainable papers are used as measured by the PREPS grading system. We undertake an annual audit to monitor our sustainability.

BRIEF CONTENTS

DETAILED CONTENTS

AUTHOR BIOGRAPHY

Charlotte Brookfield is a senior lecturer of social sciences at Cardiff University. She is based in the Cardiff Q-Step Centre of Excellence in Quantitative Methods Teaching and Learning. The Centre is one of eighteen across the UK which aim to enhance the training experience of quantitative research methods for social science students. The pedagogic activities of the Centre have influenced her research interests and, in particular, she is interested in exploring the extent to which British sociology engages with quantitative approaches and the possible factors that may contribute towards sociology students' resistance to study and use quantitative techniques.

Dr Brookfield teaches a range of research methods and substantive modules at both undergraduate and postgraduate level. Specifically, she convenes the Real World Research Placement module, where students are afforded the opportunity to put into practice the quantitative skills they have acquired in lectures in a local work organisation. Organisations involved in this module include the Welsh Government, the Welsh Blood Service and the Welsh Wheelchair Basketball Association. It was through leading this module that she came to realise the necessity for social science students and graduates to have a greater familiarity with Microsoft Excel.

In her spare time, she enjoys baking and crafting.

ACKNOWLEDGEMENTS

I would like to extend a big thank you to the team at SAGE for their support and guidance through the process of writing this book. They have been responsive and encouraging throughout, alleviating my anxieties and concerns. I would also like to thank the anonymous reviewers who have commented on both the original book proposal and various chapters along the way. Your feedback has been extremely valuable. Last but not least, I want to thank all my family, friends and colleagues who have supported me throughout this journey in their own different ways. Any errors or omissions in this book are entirely my own.

ONLINE RESOURCES

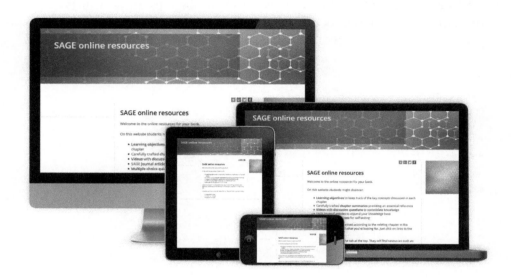

Using Microsoft Excel for Social Research is supported by a wealth of online resources. Find them at: **https://study.sagepub.com/brookfield**

For students

Video tutorials from author Charlotte Brookfield show you step-by-step how to use Excel and enable you to increase your confidence with different techniques at your own pace.

Sample datasets give you the chance to get hands-on with putting theory into practice, enabling you to try statistical techniques on real data.

Mac tips and tricks empower Mac users to get to grips with the techniques discussed in the book.

Case studies from the SAGE Research Methods platform illustrate how statistical methods are used in real research.

SAGE journal articles help you broaden your knowledge of social science and understand key themes and ideas.

For instructors

PowerPoint slides with key topics, themes and visuals from the book are available for you to customise and use in your own teaching.

A **test bank** of multiple-choice questions related to the topic of each chapter can be downloaded and used in class or as set questions to test students' understanding.

Loans

Ms Sharon Murray
13 Dec 2021

Broadmoor revealed /
Stevens, Mark
Item barcode: 3303609850
Due date: 10 Jan 2022

1

INTRODUCTION

This book is designed to help develop skills for quantitative research. Specifically, it focuses on how Microsoft Excel can be used for research projects in the social sciences. Each chapter begins with an outline which details the research methods skills covered in that chapter as well as the specific Excel skills described. The outline also includes the full name of the datasets used in the examples presented in the chapter, which allows the reader to replicate the statistical analysis discussed. All the datasets used in the book are open access and can be downloaded easily free of charge. Chapters are colour coded with 'green' chapters for beginners, 'amber' for those students with a little more experience and familiarity with quantitative research, and 'red' for those confident with the terms and techniques described elsewhere in the book. Each chapter contains at least one activity and one teaching idea. Space is provided for you to complete these activities. The teaching ideas draw on the author's own experience of teaching quantitative research methods to both pre-university and university-level social science students. Additional readings are also signposted throughout the book.

The rest of this introductory chapter makes the case for using Excel for research projects in the social sciences. It also outlines the contents of the book, so that readers can go directly to specific chapters if they wish. Key terms and Excel shortcuts are included at the end of this chapter. These key terms and shortcuts will be referred to extensively throughout the book and will be useful to return to periodically. As you use Excel with greater frequency, these terms and shortcuts will become more familiar to you.

1.1 Using Excel for Research Projects

Excel is a spreadsheet program that can be used to analyse and visualise data. While lots of statistical software packages exist, the ubiquitous nature of

Microsoft Office programs means that Excel can be a viable and important alternative (Barton and Reichow, 2012). A strong case for students and graduates to develop Excel skills has been advanced (Warner and Meehan, 2001). Many work organisations do not have expensive licences for specialised statistical software packages; however, there is often an expectation that graduates and even placement students should have a familiarity with spreadsheets and be able to undertake statistical analysis in Excel. It has also been suggested that the simplicity of the input and output of data in Excel can make the program more user friendly for those new to statistical analysis. Specifically, compared with more specialised packages, Excel does not produce as great a volume of redundant output and therefore it can be easier for users to identify key figures to report, analyse and interpret. This can mean that the analysis is much more akin to examples set out in introductory statistics textbooks, again enabling students to report and interpret their findings with more confidence. In addition to this, students often have a familiarity with Excel or, more broadly, Microsoft Office. The familiar look and menu options can help alleviate some students' fears of quantitative data analysis.

In this book, examples will be given to demonstrate how Excel can be used to undertake research projects in the social sciences. The data used in these examples can be broadly classed as social science examples and draw on topics including health, work and education. Excel 2016 is used to demonstrate the functionality of the program and its application to social science research. However, many of the techniques and formulae shown can be used on older versions of the program.

Throughout this book you will be introduced to a number of Excel formulae that can be used to undertake statistical analysis. All formulae in Excel begin with an '=' sign. Some useful operators that you will frequently see in formulae are listed in Table 1.1.

Operators often used in formulae in Excel

Table 1.1 Operators used in formulae in Microsoft Excel

Operators	Function
+	Addition
-	Subtraction
*	Multiplication
/	Division
<	Less than
>	Greater than
<=	Less than or equal to
>=	Greater than or equal to
<>	Not equal to

In this book, the term 'select' is used to describe one single left click of the mouse. When it is necessary to double click, or right click, this is clearly stated.

1.2 A Note on Teaching and Learning Statistics

Previous research has highlighted that some social science students are surprised to encounter number as part of their degree programme (Williams et al., 2008; Chamberlain et al., 2015; MacInnes, 2018a). Therefore, this book aims to highlight the relevance of statistics to studying and understanding the social world. Those students who are apprehensive (or even reluctant) to engage with such techniques may also find these additional resources helpful in increasing their confidence in using numerical approaches:

Jones, R.C. 2020. *Essential Maths Skills for Exploring Social Data*. London: Sage.

MacInnes, J. 2018b. *Little Quick Fix: Know your Numbers*. London: Sage.

1.3 Introducing the Chapters

Chapter 1: Introduction: Introducing key features of this book.

Chapter 2: Planning and Undertaking a Research Project in the Social Sciences: Considering topics for research and some of the challenges when starting a research project.

Chapter 3: Selecting, Evaluating and Cleaning Data Using Microsoft Excel: Preparing data for analysis in Excel.

Chapter 4: Getting Familiar with Your Data: Understanding and describing data using Excel.

Chapter 5: Exploring Bivariate Relationships: Crosstabulations and Chi-Square Statistic: Exploring whether respondents belong to different categories and investigating whether they are statistically significantly more likely to belong to one response category compared with another using Excel.

Chapter 6: T-tests, ANOVA and Non-parametric Equivalents: Exploring whether two independent groups are statistically significantly different using Excel.

Chapter 7: Exploring Bivariate Relationships: Correlation: Exploring the strength and direction of an association between two variables using Excel.

Chapter 8: Exploring Multivariate Relationships: Linear Regression: Similar to correlation, but exploring how three or more variables relate to each other. Investigating which variables can statistically significantly predict a particular outcome using Excel.

Chapter 9: Bringing It All Together: Writing and Presenting Research for Different Audiences: Presenting and visualising data for different audiences using Excel.

1.4 Key Words

Workbook: An Excel file.

Worksheet: A page (or sheet) in an Excel file. You may have multiple worksheets in an individual workbook.

Variable: Contains data relating to a specific quality/characteristic/attitude/belief. Datasets contain numerous variables. For example, a dataset may contain the variables highest qualification, age, weight or attitude towards school subjects.

Observation: An individual case, one respondent's data.

Rows: Observations are organised in rows. These go horizontally across the worksheet. This means all the data stored in one row belongs to one independent person. Rows are labelled numerically.

Columns: Variables are organised in columns. These go vertically down the worksheet. This means all the data stored in one column relates to a particular variable. Columns are labelled alphabetically.

Cells: Where the rows and columns meet. Each cell contains data relating to a specific participant for a specific variable.

1.5 Excel Shortcuts

CTRL+O = Open Workbook

CTRL+W = Close Workbook

CTRL+S = Save Workbook

CTRL+0 = Hide Selected Columns

CTRL+9 = Hide Selected Rows

CTRL+SHIFT+0 = Unhide Columns

CTRL+SHIFT+9 = Unhide Rows

CTRL+A = Select Entire Table

(CTRL+A)×2 = Select Entire Worksheet

CTRL+; = Insert Current Date

CTRL+: = Insert Current Time

ALT+Enter = Start New Line in Cell

ALT+H+W = Make All Text in a Cell Visible

CTRL+Spacebar = Select Entire Column

SHIFT+Spacebar = Select Entire Row

CTRL+' = Copy Formula from Cell Above

CTRL+SHIFT+" = Copy Value from Cell Above

CTRL+D = Fill Down (Fill Column)

CTRL+F = Search Worksheet

CTRL+R = Fill Right (Fill Row)

CTRL+Y = Repeat Last Entry

CTRL+ SHIFT+~ = Switch between Viewing Formulae and Values in Cells

CTRL+N = Create New Workbook

SHIFT+F11 = Insert New Worksheet

CTRL+PgDn = Go to Next Worksheet

CTRL+PgUp = Go to Previous Worksheet

2

PLANNING AND UNDERTAKING A RESEARCH PROJECT IN THE SOCIAL SCIENCES

Considering topics for research and some of the challenges when starting a research project

Colour Code for Chapter:
Green
Study Skills:
Planning, Time management, Thinking ethically
Research Methods Skills:
Research ethics, Research management
Microsoft Excel Skills:
Creating a Gantt chart

Visit **https://study.sagepub.com/brookfield** to download the datasets used in this chapter.

Chapter Outline

This chapter will describe some of the key criteria to consider when designing and developing a research project. It will include guidance on how to plan effectively and undertake a research project and also guidance on how Excel can be used to help visualise the research process and plan a project. The chapter will also encourage readers to think about the potential ethical implications of their proposed research and to consider their own positionality in the research project.

2.1 Introduction

Often knowing where to start with a research project can be the most overwhelming phase. In some instances, you may be given a particular research title or problem to explore. However, despite the aims and the objectives of the research being stipulated, it is still down to you to make some important decisions during the research process. Equally, in such scenarios, it is important to plan a research project carefully to ensure that you can achieve the required aims in the time set aside. In other instances, you may be given an even larger degree of flexibility and be able to choose freely a research project or theme to explore that is of interest to you. This responsibility can be daunting, even for those who are particularly keen to research a specific topic in more depth. But what do you do if you have no ideas on what to research? Or what if you are unsure whether your project is viable? This chapter highlights some of the key considerations that researchers should be mindful of when selecting a research project. It also suggests sources of inspiration for research projects, for those who are unsure what to research.

2.2 Sources of Inspiration for Research Projects

When deciding what to research, there are some key factors that you can consider.

2.2.1 Future ambitions

Can you research a topic relating to the profession or career that you wish to pursue? Researching an issue that is of relevance and interest to potential employers can prove helpful when writing job applications and during job interviews. Alternatively, if you wish to pursue a further qualification, is it possible to begin to explore some of the key topics that you will be taught? This will help towards demonstrating your genuine passion and interest to the discipline or topic that you have chosen.

2.2.2 Contemporary issues

Is there a contemporary issue in the media that you could research further and find out more about? Looking at a contemporary issue can really engage both the researcher and any research participants. The relevance and timelessness of research can motivate people to partake in research and can enhance the quality of the data collected.

2.2.3 Previous learning

Is there a topic that you previously studied, but want to know more about? If there was a topic that you covered in a previous module that you particularly enjoyed, this can be a good starting point for a research project. Consider what else you would like to know about the topic. A strong interest and enthusiasm for a research project can help motivate you to keep going. Alternatively, is there something you know a lot about, or perhaps a topic that you were previously assessed on and received a high mark for? As university research projects can carry a lot of module credits and be both time and labour intensive, it can be advantageous to consider your strengths before commencing a project and play to these.

2.2.4 Hobbies and interests

Do you have any particular hobbies or interests? What academic research has been done on these? Again, exploring and building upon previous research surrounding a personal hobby or interest can help maintain your enthusiasm and motivation for a project. In addition to this, if you require participants for your research it is likely that you will already have some contacts willing to contribute to your project.

2.3 Six Tips for Getting off to a Good Start

2.3.1 Familiarise yourself with your course requirements

It is important to familiarise yourself with any requirements that you may need to fulfil as part of your university course. In particular, if your degree programme is accredited by a professional body, there may be specific requirements in relation to data collection. Regardless of this, it is important to ascertain the following information prior to commencing your project. When does the project need to be completed? How long does the project need to be and what is included/excluded from this word count? In what format should the research be presented? How should the research project be submitted?

2.3.2 Plan your time effectively

Before starting a research project, note the end date. What is the deadline for this project? And does it coincide with any other commitments or approaching deadlines? For instance, you may have other university modules that you are completing along-side your research project. Also ensure that you allocate sufficient time for data collection. Consider not only how long it may take to recruit participants and collect data, but also other factors, such as whether there are potentially unsuitable times for participants to take part in your research. For instance, if you are researching in schools, be mindful of when the academic term starts and finishes and be aware of the exam season.

2.3.3 Use your supervisor

In most instances, when undertaking a research project, you will be assigned a supervisor. It is important that you speak to your supervisor about all aspects of your research project and get regular feedback on the work that you are producing. While models of supervision vary across institutions and, indeed, even within institutions, it is key to arrive to supervision meetings prepared. Send work in advance of meetings. This will give your supervisor sufficient time to read and comment on your work. Secondly, try to prepare a list of questions for your meeting. This can be particularly important when you have limited time or meeting opportunities with your supervisor. These questions will guide the conversation with your supervisor and ensure that you get the most out of your meeting. It is important to remember that your supervisor may be overseeing a number of student projects; therefore it is essential that you establish at the outset reasonable deadlines that work for both of you. Also, with this in mind, ensure that you allow your supervisor adequate and reasonable time to respond to queries in relation to your project.

When you are undertaking a work-based placement project as part of your univer-sity studies, you may also be assigned a supervisor or mentor within the organisation where you are working. Sometimes, this person may have more of a pastoral role as opposed to being able to help and support you with your research project. In this instance, it is important that you identify a contact within the organisation, or within your own university, who you can approach for advice and guidance on undertaking your research.

2.3.4 Speak to others

Prior to starting research, it can be very useful to speak to others to help you refine your thinking and the focus of your project. For example, you may want to speak to friends and family about your initial ideas. It may also be worthwhile speaking to 'informed experts' – people who fit the demographic that you wish to research, or have experience working with the groups which you want to investigate. By speaking to these experts, you will gain a better idea of the feasibility of your study and they may be able to help you identify the research priorities and gaps in existing knowledge and understanding.

2.3.5 Look at example projects

Many universities will have copies of research projects from previous cohorts available for students to look at. Looking at these can help you gain a better insight into what you are expected to achieve and also be a source of inspiration. If you do look at example projects, make sure that you do not plagiarise other people's work. Plagiarism, or copying someone else's work, is seen as a serious form of academic dishonesty.

As well as student projects, it may be advantageous to look at research studies published in relevant journals for your discipline. You may decide to adopt the methodology of an existing study but explore the phenomena with a more contemporary or different sample or in a different location. Again, it is important that you properly acknowledge these academic studies by using both in-text citations and correctly referencing the relevant study in the bibliography.

2.3.6 Think small

It is important to be mindful of the time and resource limitations that surround your project. Make sure that the research project you pick is manageable and feasible. It is often the case that first-time researchers will have grand plans for their research, when in reality they do not have sufficient time, resources, access and/or expertise to undertake this level of research. With big, broad topics it can also be difficult to know where to begin and what to omit when writing up the research. As such, it is important to be mindful and frank about limitations in time, resources, access and expertise at the start of a research project and to choose something that you can successfully see through from beginning to end.

2.4 Planning a Research Project: Who/What, Where, Why and How?

When designing a research project, you need to develop something both original and practical. Therefore, it can be useful to ask yourself the following questions before you get started:

- *Who/What:* Who or what is it that you want to research?
- *Where:* Where will you carry out this research? Is it a safe place? Can you realistically access this place? Is this an appropriate space for you and your participants to undertake the research?
- *Why:* Why is this research important? Is it an issue that is in the news? Is it an issue that has been overlooked in previous academic literature? Is it an issue that relates to your own interests and/or career plans?
- *How:* How are you going to research this topic? Are you going to collect primary or use secondary data? Are you going to use quantitative or qualitative methods? Are you realistically going to be able to access the data you need in the allocated time?

It is important to include all this information in any research proposals that you develop. Thinking about these issues at the start of a project can save time later on.

2.5 The Research Process

The research process involves several steps. At the beginning of the process, it is necessary to identify the problem or issue that needs to be investigated. It is then important to familiarise yourself with what is already known about this issue. This can be done by looking at research that has already been conducted in the area. At this stage, you may begin to identify gaps in the existing literature. For instance, is what we already know about the research problem somewhat dated? Is all the existing research based in one country? Has the existing literature only explored the proposed research problem with a particular demographic? By considering how your research fills a gap in the existing literature you can help demonstrate the necessity and originality of the work you intend to carry out.

After reviewing the existing literature surrounding your chosen research topic, you then need to consider the most appropriate methods for this study. Again, it is important when thinking about this to consider the time and resource implications of different methods of data collection and also to address any ethical concerns associated with a particular mode of data collection (see Section 2.6 below). You need to ensure that your study participants will engage with your method of data collection and that it is appropriate for investigating the topic.

Once you have collected your data, the process of analysis begins. Often it is necessary to clean your dataset before analysis can commence (see Section 3.14). The main findings of your analysis need to be clearly reported, using tables, charts and graphs to help visualise your results (see Chapter 9). After this, your findings need to be discussed in relation to the wider, existing literature. It is important at this stage to start to consider the implications of your findings on policy and/or practice.

The final stage of a research project usually involves reflecting on the key findings and the strengths and limitations of the study. At this stage, it may also be useful to consider ideas for future research based on the findings of the current project. This research process is represented graphically in Figure 2.1.

Figure 2.1   The research process

While this description presents the research process as linear and sequential, in actuality it is often much messier and iterative. For instance, many researchers feel the need to revisit their literature review after collecting their data, as a result of new or unexpected themes arising. Equally, while considering the methodological approach for the study, it can be the case that researchers begin to recognise some of the limitations of their work and begin to note these down to include in their conclusion.

2.6 Being an Ethical Researcher

Thinking about and taking action to reduce or, where possible, remove any ethical issues associated with a research project is both responsible and moral. At the start of a project, it is important to consider any potential ethical considerations associated with the research project. This process involves reflecting on any potential harms that research participants or the researcher may encounter. After considering these harms, it is necessary to outline steps that will be taken to minimise these. The Economic Social Research Council outlines six key principles to undertaking ethical social science research, as follows:

- research should aim to maximise benefit for individuals and society and minimise risk and harm
- the rights and dignity of individuals and groups should be respected
- wherever possible, participation should be voluntary and appropriately informed
- research should be conducted with integrity and transparency
- lines of responsibility and accountability should be clearly defined
- independence of research should be maintained and where conflicts of interest cannot be avoided they should be made explicit. (ESRC, 2019)

Most institutions will have a formal ethical clearance process that you will be required to go through before commencing a research project. In most instances, this will involve your having to outline your research project and identify potential harms to both the researcher and any participants. You will also need to consider carefully how you will store, anonymise and, later, destroy any raw data collected. It is important to think carefully about the questions that you ask your research participants and exclude any unnecessary questions. Not only will unnecessary questions make a survey longer and potentially lead to greater dropout, but also unnecessary questions could compromise the anonymity of the participants. Each institution will have a bespoke process for applying for ethical clearance and it is important that you familiarise yourself with this process and allow adequate time for the process when planning a project.

If you are carrying out research in an external organisation, it will have its own policies and practices surrounding data protection and security. It is important to speak to the relevant people within the organisation to ensure that you do not breach these policies. It may be that you are required to attend mandatory training before being given access to a company's data.

2.7 Being Reflexive

Being a reflexive researcher involves careful consideration of how your own background and values may have influenced the research decisions that you have made. While the concept is often under-utilised in quantitative research, Ryan and Golden (2006) make the case for quantitative researchers to reflect upon how their own attitudes, beliefs and preconceived ideas may have impacted on the research process.

2.8 Using a Gantt Chart to Plan Your Time
2.8.1 Creating a Gantt chart

A Gantt chart is a visual representation which shows both the duration of time that discrete parts of a project should take to complete and the sequence in which different tasks will be undertaken to ensure the project is completed to schedule. It is good practice to create a Gantt chart at the start of a research project to ensure that you plan your time effectively. Gantt charts can be created in Excel. Before creating a Gantt chart, it is important to identify the key components of your research project. A generic list is displayed below:

- Research proposal
- Research ethics application
- Literature review
- Methodology
- Data collection
- Data analysis
- Discussion
- Conclusion

When creating a Gantt chart, you also need to consider carefully how long each individual part of the project will take. Some tasks, such as collecting your data, can be a very lengthy process and, in some instances, particularly when you are working to a deadline, you may decide to complete more than one task at a time. For instance, you may choose to finish writing your methodology chapter while you begin the data collection process. Although the Gantt chart provides some structure to the research process, it is important to remember that good researchers need to be able to think flexibly. The research process is often not a linear one and research can be postponed throughout the process. For instance, gatekeepers may not get back to researchers in a timely manner causing them to have to change plans.

2.8.2 Creating a Gantt Chart in Excel

It is possible to make Gantt charts in Excel. To do this, begin by creating a table with the column headings **Tasks**, **Start Date** and **Number of Days**.

Under the '**Tasks**' heading, list all the aspects of the project that you need to undertake. This may include activities such as literature review, data collection and data analysis.

In the column titled '**Start Date**', insert the date on which you intend to start each task (e.g. literature review, data collection and data analysis). The dates must be formatted as dd/mm/yyyy.

In the final column ('**Number of Days**'), enter the number of days that you plan to spend on each task.

Table 2.1 demonstrates this. It is important also to include an overall project start date in a separate cell on the worksheet. In the example shown in Table 2.1, the overall project start date has been inserted in cell G1.

Table 2.1 Example table used to make a Gantt chart in Microsoft Excel

	A	B	C	D	E	F	G
1	Tasks	Start Date	Number of Days			Project Start Date:	08/10/2019
2	Background research	08/10/2019	14				
3	Literature review	20/10/2019	14				
4	Formulating hypotheses	19/10/2019	3				
5	Data collection	22/10/2019	7				
6							
7							
8							
9							
10							

Once you have entered this data you can begin to create the Gantt chart. To begin, click '**Insert**' and, under the '**Charts**' menu, select a 2-D Stacked Bar chart (Figure 2.2). This will initially create a white rectangle. Note that it is important that none of the cells containing data are selected at this point.

Insert > Charts > 2-D Stacked Bar chart

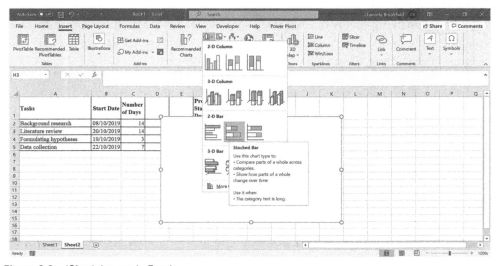

Figure 2.2 '**Charts**' menu in Excel

Right click inside the white rectangle and choose '**Select Data**' from the drop-down menu. This will open a new window (Figure 2.3).

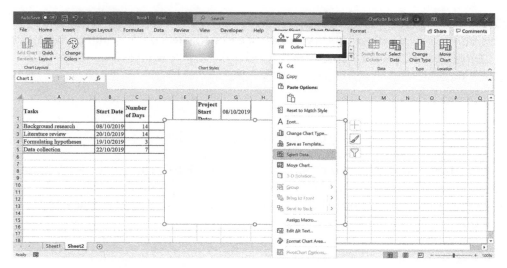

Figure 2.3   Select Data option in Excel

Under '**Legend Entries (Series)**', select '**Add**'. A new window will open titled '**Edit Series**'.

For the '**Series Name**' select the column heading '**Start Date**'; in this example (Figure 2.4), cell B1. In the box '**Series Values**', select and highlight the '**Start Date**' column, *excluding the column heading*. In this example, this would be cells B2 to B5. Click **OK**.

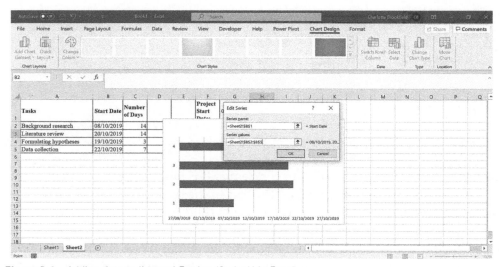

Figure 2.4   Adding data to 'Legend Entries (Series)' in Excel

Series Name=Start Date column heading

Series Values=Start Date column (excluding column heading)

Under '**Legend Entries (Series)**' select '**Add**' again and repeat the process; however, this time select '**Number of Days**' as the '**Series Name**' and the column '**Number of Days**' for the '**Series Values**'. In this example, cell C1 would be the 'Series Name' and the 'Series Values' would be cells C2 to C5.

Series Name=Number of Days column heading

Series Values=Number of Days column (excluding column heading)

Under '**Horizontal (Category) Axis Labels**', click '**Edit**'. Then select and highlight the column of '**Tasks**' (excluding the column head). In this instance (Figure 2.5), this would be cells A2 to A5. Click '**OK'** to close the windows and you will be able to see your Gantt chart.

Horizontal (Category) Axis Labels > Edit > Highlight Tasks (excluding column heading) > OK

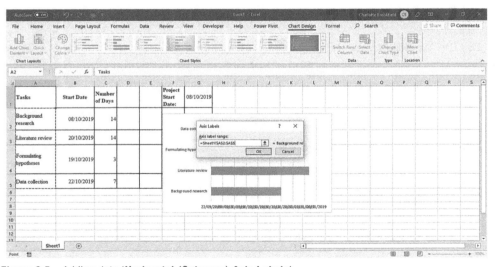

Figure 2.5 Adding data '**Horizontal (Category) Axis Labels**'

You may need to resize your chart to ensure that it is fully visible. At this point, the bars will be appearing in two colours. The bars in the second colour (on the right of the graph) are the ones that are needed for the Gantt chart. Each of these bars (in the second colour) represents the duration of time that is devoted to each task and where the bar begins dictates when the task should start. It is necessary to remove the coloured fill from the first bar. This will make it easier to read your Gantt chart. To do this, click one of the bars filled with the first colour and, under '**Fill**', select '**No Fill**' (Figure 2.6).

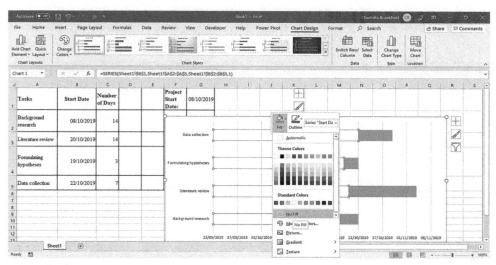

Figure 2.6   Coloured fill being removed from Gantt chart bars in Excel

At this point, you may also notice that the final tasks in your project are listed at the top of your Gantt chart, with tasks that should take place earlier in the research process appearing at the bottom of the chart. To reverse this, right click the task labels in the Gantt chart. Then, select '**Format Axis**' and from the menu select the option '**Categories in reverse order**' (Figure 2.7).

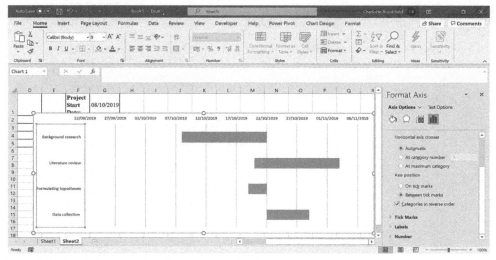

Figure 2.7   Reversing the order of categories in Excel

Finally, click the cell which contains the '**Project Start Date**'. In this example, this is cell G1. Change the format of that cell from '**Date**' to '**Number**' (see Figure 2.8). This can be done using the drop-down menu on the main top toolbar. You will notice that Excel automatically recognises that you have entered a date; however, for the purposes of making the Gantt chart you need to override this and change the date into number format.

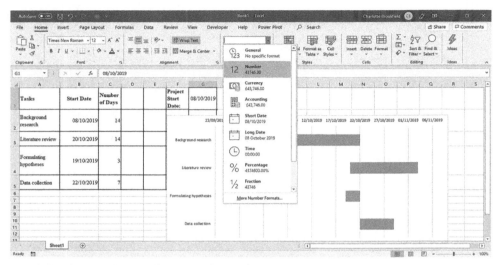

Figure 2.8 Changing '**Project Start Date**' to '**Number**'

Right click the dates in your Gantt chart and select '**Format Axis**'. Under axis options, change the minimum value to the number that now appears in the project start date cell (G1 in Figure 2.9). This will complete your Gantt chart.

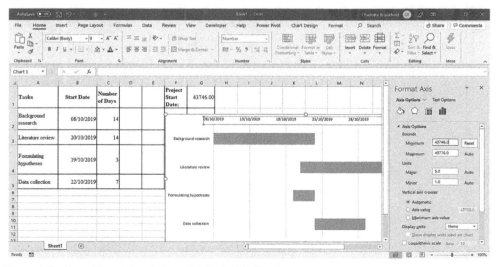

Figure 2.9 Formatting date axis for a Gantt chart in Excel

Activity

Plan a Research Project

Use Table 2.2 to help you plan an effective research project. Make notes of all the ideas that come into your head and some of the practical constraints that you may need to consider.

Table 2.2   Planning a research project: who/what, where, why and how?

Project Ideas	Who/What	Where	Why	How
Idea 1				
Idea 2				
Idea 3				

Create a Gantt Chart

Create a Gantt chart in Excel for your chosen research project. Remember to consider carefully the deadline for your project and check whether you have any other commitments that you should be mindful of when planning how you will spend your time. It is a good idea to share this Gantt chart with your supervisor. This way you can agree convenient times for them to look at your work and give you feedback. They can also advise whether you have allocated sufficient time for each task.

Further Reading

ESRC. 2019. *Our Core Principles*. Available at: https://esrc.ukri.org/funding/guidance-for-applicants/research-ethics/our-core-principles/ [Accessed 30 July 2019].

Grey, D. 2018. *Doing Research in the Real World*, 5th edn. London: Sage.

Ryan, L. and Golden, A. 2006. 'Tick the Box Please': A Reflexive Approach to Doing Quantitative Social Research. *Sociology* 40(6), pp. 1191–2000.

Skills Checklist for Chapter 2

Use the checklist below to track your learning and to highlight areas where you may need to do some additional reading.

	I can do this confidently	I could do this if I had a little more practice	I need more help with this
Consider the ethical implications of a research project			
Plan a research project			
Think reflexively about a research project			
Create a Gantt chart to help manage my time			

Ideas for Teachers/Instructors

The Research Process Challenge

Set your students the challenge of going through the entire research process in 30 minutes to try and answer a predefined research question. The research question can be related to a contemporary topical issue or can be a more frivolous example such as, 'What do students eat for breakfast?' Give the students five minutes to review the literature on the topic, five minutes to design an interview schedule and/or survey, five minutes to collect data from their peers, five minutes to analyse their data and five minutes to reflect on their findings. Once they have gone through this process, get them to discuss whether they encountered any issues and to reflect on the quality of their literature review, data collection and data analysis. Ask the students which aspects of the research process they would spend five more minutes on if they had extra time.

This exercise should give your students a 'flavour' of all the different stages of the research process and highlight some of the potential challenges and pitfalls of researching. It will also demonstrate to your students the necessity to plan and carefully consider the timings of a research project. It may also reinforce the idea that research is an iterative process. For instance, there may be someone in the classroom who raises an idea that a student did not consider in their initial review of the literature.

3

SELECTING, EVALUATING AND CLEANING DATA USING MICROSOFT EXCEL

Preparing data for analysis in Microsoft Excel

Colour Code for Chapter:
Green
Study Skills:
Referencing a dataset, Evaluating data
Research Methods Skills:
Preparing and cleaning data, Validity, Reliability
Microsoft Excel Skills:
Vlookup, Hlookup, Concatenate, Freeze Panes, Filter Data, Cronbach's Alpha, Data Validation
Datasets Used:
European Quality of Life Time Series, 2007 and 2011: Open Access
Living Costs and Food Survey, 2013: Unrestricted Access Teaching Dataset
Opinions and Lifestyle Survey, Well-Being Module, January, February, April and May, 2015
Public Attitudes to Animal Research Survey, 2016
Quarterly Labour Force Survey Household Dataset, January–March, 2015

Visit **https://study.sagepub.com/brookfield** to download the datasets used in this chapter.

─**Chapter Outline**─

This chapter will direct readers to possible sources of data that can be used for quantitative data projects. It will also provide criteria on how to assess the quality of a dataset and some guidance on how to 'clean' data in Excel before commencing statistical analysis.

3.1 Introduction

There is a wealth of data readily available to researchers. This chapter will highlight some key sources of data that can be used to carry out quantitative social research. The chapter will also describe how you can evaluate and clean data. It is important to prepare data carefully before you begin to analyse it. This can be a lengthy process; however, it can improve the quality of your findings and increase your familiarity with the dataset, including the strengths and limitations of the data.

3.2 Columns and Rows

It is important to be able to differentiate between columns and rows when undertaking quantitative data analysis. Columns go up and down a spreadsheet or table, while rows go across. Usually each column in a dataset represents a different variable and each row represents a different case, person or observation. In Excel, columns are referred to using letters, while rows are referred to using numbers. When referring to particular cells in a spreadsheet, it is commonplace to use the column letter followed

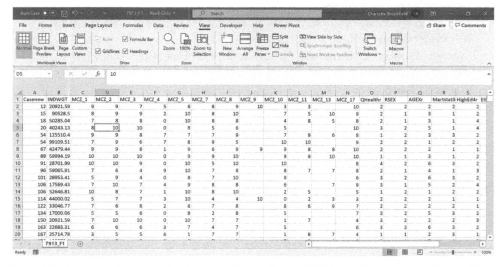

Figure 3.1 Data extract from the Opinions and Lifestyle Survey, Well-Being Module (April and May, 2015)

by the row number to describe the cell under discussion. For example, in the extract of data from the Opinions and Lifestyle Survey, Well-Being Module (April and May, 2015) shown in Figure 3.1, the cell D5 tells us the value for the variable **MCZ_2** (Overall, to what extent do you feel that the things you do in your life are worthwhile?) for the case ID number '20'. In this situation, respondent 20 has given a value of 10 for the variable **MCZ_2**. This is the highest possible response value for this question, thus suggesting that respondent 20 strongly believes that the things they do in their life are worthwhile.

3.3 Sources of Data

In the social world there is so much data that has already been collected and that researchers can access and use. This data is often overlooked, with researchers opting to collect their own data rather than taking advantage of the resources already available. Below is a list of different web sources where existing datasets can be accessed.

- **UK Data Service** (https://www.ukdataservice.ac.uk/): The UK Data Service is funded by the Economic and Social Research Council and is the UK's largest collection of social science and humanities datasets. It contains mostly UK datasets, but it also contains some international datasets. Some of the datasets have been simplified and cleaned for teaching purposes, for example the Quarterly Labour Force Survey (January–March, 2015) and the Living Costs and Food Survey (2013). These have unrestricted access, meaning that they can be accessed freely without the need for creating a user profile. These can be useful resources for practising and refining your data analysis skills.
- **Office for National Statistics** (https://www.ons.gov.uk): The Office for National Statistics is the national statistical institute for the UK. It has local, regional and national data on a range of topics.
- **UK Government Data** (https://data.gov.uk): The UK government shares open access data collected by local authorities and central government.
- **StatsWales** (https://statswales.gov.wales): An online data repository specifically for Welsh government data. The available data covers a range of themes including housing, health and sustainability.
- **Eurostat** (http://ec.europa.eu/eurostat): Eurostat is the statistical office of the European Union. It provides data at the European level in order to enable comparisons between EU countries and regions.
- **Data.gov** (https://www.data.gov): Data.gov contains open US government data on a range of topics including consumerism, health, agriculture and public safety.

- **Data.gov.au** (https://data.gov.au): Data.gov.au contains open source data from Australia on themes such as education, crime and policing. The data includes open government data as well as data from academic research and from research institutions.
- **Research Data Australia** (https://researchdata.edu.au): Research Data Australia contains quantitative and qualitative data sources from government, research organisations and institutions on various topics for different academic disciplines.
- **United Nations Statistics Division** (https://unstats.un.org/home/): The United Nations Statistics Division brings together global data on a range of topics including population, poverty and health.
- **UNESCO Institute for Statistics** (http://uis.unesco.org): UNESCO Institute for Statistics provides international data on the following themes: Education and Literacy; Science, Technology and Innovation; Culture and Communication, and Information.
- **World Bank Open Data** (https://data.worldbank.org): World Bank Open Data allows you to search for data either by country or by indicator. It includes data on agriculture, education and poverty as well as many other themes.
- **SAGE Research Methods Datasets** (https://uk.sagepub.com/en-gb/eur/sage-research-methods-datasets): The SAGE Research Methods Datasets are datasets that have been created especially for teaching and learning research methods. The datasets cover topics in psychology, education, sociology and many more.

In recent years, there has been a proliferation of data routinely collected and stored as part of everyday life (Burrows and Savage, 2014; Savage and Burrows, 2007). Some of this data is publicly available for researchers to access and use. For instance:

- **Uber Movement Data** (https://movement.uber.com/?lang=en-GB): A database of anonymised Uber journeys across the globe.
- **Unistats Data** (https://www.hesa.ac.uk/support/tools-and-downloads/unistats): Data that enables researchers to compare different degree programmes offered in different higher education institutions.

3.4 Referencing a Dataset

It is important to remember to reference a dataset that you use in any work that you produce. If you do not reference a dataset, your analysis cannot be replicated, and this can jeopardise the reliability of your work (see Section 3.14.2). Equally, not referencing a dataset is a form of plagiarism, something that is deemed very poor practice and unethical in academia. By referencing the dataset, credit is attributed to the original author and the reader is able to return to the dataset and conduct further analysis if they wish to.

To reference a dataset, you need the following information:

- Author(s)/creator(s)
- Date of publication
- Title of dataset
- Data repository, date accessed
- Digital object identifier (DOI)

The final reference, formatted in Harvard referencing style, should look like this:

> Author(s)/Creator(s). (Date of Publication). *Title of dataset*, [data collection], Data Repository, Date Accessed. Digital Object Identifier.

For instance, if you wanted to reference the *GP Patient Survey 2018*, you would report the following in the bibliography:

> NHS England. (2018). *The GP Patient Survey 2018*, [data collection], UK Data Service, Accessed 4 June 2019. http://doi.org/10.5255/UKDA-SN-853308.

If you were using the British Election Study 2010: Campaign Internet Data in your work, you would reference the dataset in your bibliography as:

> Whiteley, P.F., Saunders, D. (2014). *British Election Study 2010: Campaign Internet Data*, [data collection], UK Data Service, Accessed 4 June 2019. http://doi.org/10.5255/UKDA-SN-7530-1.

Including the Digital Object Identifier (doi) in the reference ensures that other researchers are able to locate the exact version of the dataset that you used in your analysis.

It is important to note that different disciplines, academic institutions, research centres and even publishers use different referencing styles. Typically, the social sciences use the Harvard referencing style demonstrated here; however, it is important to confirm which style your institution uses.

Activity

Compare Countries

Pick two countries in the European Union. Use the data provided in the Eurostat database (http://ec.europa.eu/eurostat/data/database) to compare the two countries. Consider comparing the countries in relation to levels of crime, education and housing conditions.

(Continued)

Complete the table with the statistics that you find. Try to include information on how the frequencies for each variable have been measured in each country.

Table 3.1 Using Eurostat data to compare two European Union countries

Variables:	Country 1:	Country 2:	How the variable was measured in country 1	How the variable was measured in country 2
Level of Crime				
Education				
Housing				

3.5 Getting Started with Excel

3.5.1 Installing the Analysis ToolPak

Excel has an add-in which makes it much quicker and easier to carry out statistical analysis. This add-in is called the '**Analysis ToolPak**'. It can be installed by using the following steps:

File > Options > Add-Ins

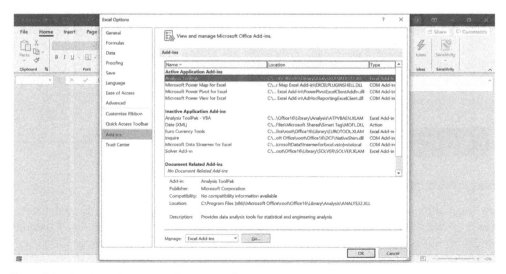

Figure 3.2 Installing the **Analysis ToolPak** in Excel

After this, select '**Analysis ToolPak**' and change the Manage option to '**Excel Add-ins**'. Click **Go…** and ensure that there is a tick next to the Analysis ToolPak option, then click **OK** (see Figure 3.2).

Once the **Analysis ToolPak** has been installed, a new option called '**Data**' will appear on the top toolbar.

3.5.2 Data coding

The process of inputting data into a spreadsheet is often referred to as coding. This is because the process involves the researcher attributing different numerical values (or codes) to different response categories or options. For example, when looking at the variable 'Economic Position of Household Reference Person' (**A093r**) from the Living Costs and Food Survey (2013), the information in the survey guidance explains that the variable is coded as in Table 3.2.

Table 3.2 Coding for variable *A093r* from the Living Costs and Food Survey (2013)

Coding for Variable: Economic Position of Household Reference Person	
Response Category	Code
Full-time working	1
Part-time working	2
Unemployed and work related Government training programmes	3
Economically inactive	4

This means that a respondent who answered '1' is in full-time work, whereas a respondent who answered '4' is economically inactive.

When coding data, it is important to ensure that the categories are mutually exclusive. A participant's response can only be given one code, and as such each category must be distinct and truly reflect the response given. Equally, in order to ensure that all responses can be coded it is important to have a full and extensive list of codes that covers all possibilities. In some situations, it may be advantageous to code responses that do not fit into the main list of codes as 'Other'.

3.6 Dealing with Non-numerical Values

Occasionally, when working with pre-existing data, Excel may not recognise values entered in a spreadsheet as numerical values. In these situations, when you begin to analyse your data, you will get an error message explaining that non-numerical data has been entered.

To overcome this problem and to enable Excel to recognise the response values as numerical data, you need to use the Paste Special function. To begin, type the number '1' into an empty cell and then right click and select '**Copy**' (alternatively, you can use the keyboard shortcut CTRL+C to copy the number). Then, highlight the column that you wish to convert to numeric values. After this, in the '**Home**' tab, select the drop-down menu beneath '**Paste**' and choose the option '**Paste Special**' (see Figure 3.3). This will open a new window.

Copy > Paste > Paste Special

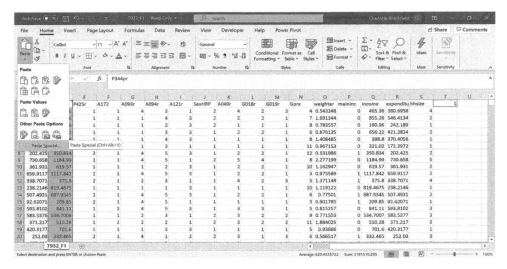

Figure 3.3   Using '**Paste Special**' to deal with non-numerical values in Excel

In the new window, under '**Operation**', select '**Multiply**' and then click **OK**. Excel will now recognise your data as numeric.

3.7 Vlookup

The Vlookup function in Excel finds and reports values that have been coded in a vertical table. For instance, when entering data manually into a spreadsheet, a researcher may wish to use shorthand or code to denote certain responses. This can help speed up the process of inputting data and reduces the possibility of error when entering data because the researcher has less to type. However, once this shorthand code has been entered, researchers, particularly if they are working collaboratively, may wish to enter the full response label or name. Alternatively, a researcher may have one spreadsheet with details of employees and their job grades and a separate table with the hourly rate of pay for each grade. In order to calculate how much each individual employee should be paid per hour, the researcher would use the Vlookup function. In this instance, the Vlookup function would use the information provided in the spreadsheet regarding job grade and find the corresponding information relating to pay in the separate table.

In the following example, the age category variable from the European Quality of Life (2007) survey is used. The guidance document that supports this dataset details the numeric response that has been given to each age category. This information can be entered into Excel and used to add textual labels to the existing numerical data. Figure 3.4 shows the age category variable and a small table that has been inserted with the textual label that each numerical response for this variable denotes. Importantly, the numerical value is in the first column of the table, while the second column includes the textual labels.

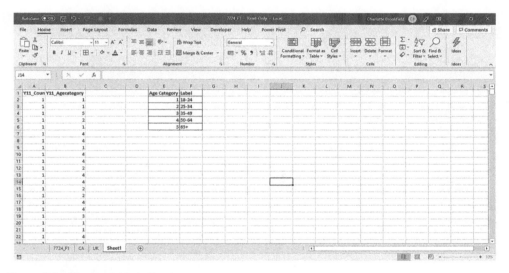

Figure 3.4   Vlookup table in Excel

To add a column next to the age category variable with the textual label, you can use the Vlookup function. In the column adjacent to the age category variable, begin by typing '=VLOOKUP'. Following this, you will need to insert an open bracket '('. You then need either to type the reference for the cell that you wish to obtain the textual label for, or to select it by clicking it. In this example, if we were interested in the age category label for the first respondent in the spreadsheet, we would begin by typing '=VLOOKUP(B2'. This needs to be followed by a comma and then the reference for the look-up table (this is known as the table array), or in other words the references for the cells that contain the data values and textual labels. In this example, this would be cells E1 to F6. This is then added to the formula to make '=VLOOKUP(B2, E1:F6'. It is important that you lock these cells by either pressing F4 or inserting dollar signs either side of the letter coordinates of the reference table ($E$1:$F$6). Locking the cells enables you to copy the formula and not lose the coordinates of the reference table. After inserting the coordinates of the table, you need to tell Excel which column in the table contains the information that you wish to insert in your spreadsheet. Here, the textual data that we need is recorded in column 2. This means that the formula now reads '=VLOOKUP(B2, $E$1:$F$6, 2'. Finally, you need to type either 'True' or 'False'. False is used in instances where an exact match is required. Alternatively, True can be used in instances where only approximation is needed. The latter may be used with test scores and grade bands. In this instance, Excel would calculate the closest grade band based on the test score (see example in Hlookup below). This means that the complete formula in this example would be '=VLOOKUP(B2, $E$1:$F$6, 2, FALSE)'. Once the formula has been entered, the brackets need to be closed and the formula can be dragged down and copied into all cells in a column. Figure 3.5 shows the formula being used.

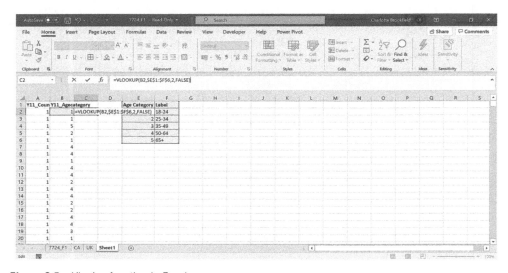

Figure 3.5   Vlookupfunction in Excel

3.8 Hlookup

Similar to Vlookup, the Hlookup function in Excel allows users to insert values from a table into a spreadsheet. In the following example, the variable **Y11_Q7** (How many hours do you normally work per week in your main job?) from the European Quality of Life (2007) survey is used. The variable is a continuous-level variable (see Section 4.2) with a range of responses. For our analysis we want to group respondents into different categories with textual labels. Specifically, we are going to look at those respondents who reported working and label them according to whether they reported working on average a low, medium or high number of hours per week. In this example, we have produced a horizontal table which defines which textual label should be associated with the number of hours normally worked. As the table is horizontal, we need to use the Hlookup function as opposed to the Vlookup function. The data and the horizontal table can be seen in Figure 3.6. The numerical values (which you will be looking up) need to be in the top row of the table and the textual labels in a latter row.

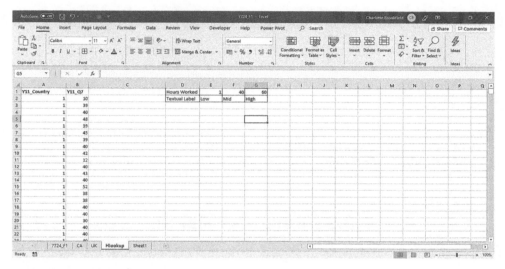

Figure 3.6 Hlookuptable in Excel

To use the Hlookup function, you begin by typing '=HLOOKUP'. Following this, you enter the reference cell. The reference cell is the cell that you wish to 'look up' in your horizontal table. In the example in Figure 3.7, the formula would appear as '=HLOOKUP(B2,'. This means that Excel will look up in which category of the reference table the value in cell B2 falls. In this example, it is seeing whether the value of '10' in cell B2 means that a respondent has worked a 'low', 'medium' or 'high' number of hours per week. This is followed by the coordinates of the horizontal reference table. It is important to lock the cell references when entering the table coordinates either using the F4 key or by inserting $ signs. Locking the cells allows you to copy the formula but not lose the coordinates for the look-up table. For this example, the formula would now look like this: '=HLOOKUP(B2, $D$1:$G$2,'. After this, you need to tell Excel which row of the table it should be reporting. In the example, the row being reported is '**Textual Label**', the second row in the table, and therefore '2' is entered in the formula. Finally, the formula needs to include true or false to denote whether Excel should be returning exact or approximate values (see the example of false in Vlookup). In this example, true is used as the horizontal table does not include exact values. This means that Excel calculates which group (low, medium or high) each respondent belongs to based upon the reported number of hours that they work. The final formula appears like this: '=HLOOKUP(B2, $D$1:$G$2, 2, TRUE)' (see Figure 3.7).

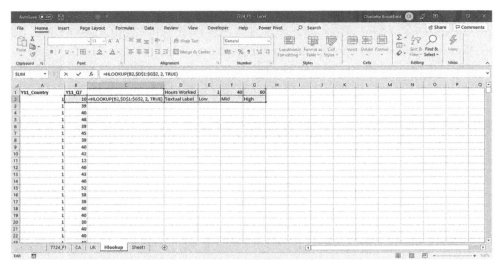

Figure 3.7   Hlookupfunction in Excel

3.9 Index and Match

In some instances, we may be interested in quickly exploring how one respondent answered a survey item. In this situation, we can use the Index function. This allows you quickly to identify a value in a cell based on a particular row or column of interest. This function would be particularly helpful in instances where there is a lot of data and it is hard to see all the columns and rows at one given time.

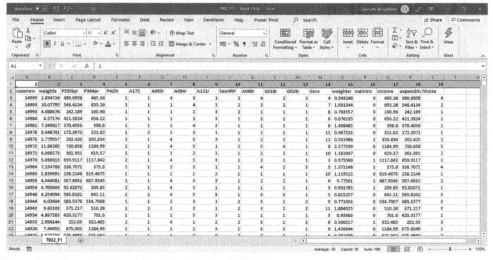

Figure 3.8   Preparing to use the Index function in Excel

Before using the Index function, it can be helpful to add a row of numbers above the first row of the dataset (the one that usually contains variable names). For instance, Figure 3.8 shows how a row of numbers has been inserted above the variable names.

We can now use the Index function to explore how specific respondents answered the survey. For example, when using the Living Costs and Food Survey (2013), we may be interested in knowing how the participant assigned the random case number (**CASENEW**) 14976 responded to the gross normal weekly household income question (**P344pr**). Usually a researcher would have reason for wanting to look at a respondent's data like this in more detail.

To use the Index function to find out the gross normal weekly household income of respondent 14976, you would need to enter the following formula '=INDEX(Table Range, Row Reference, Column Reference)'. If we were specifically interested in respondent 14976's answer, the row reference would be substituted with the number 8 and the column reference would be substituted with number 4. This is because the data belonging to participant 14976 is in row 8 and the variable **P344pr** is situated in the fourth column in the spreadsheet. Therefore, the formula would appear as '=INDEX(A:S, 8, 4)'. Essentially, Excel is telling you the value in Table A:S where row 8 meets column 4 (see Figure 3.9).

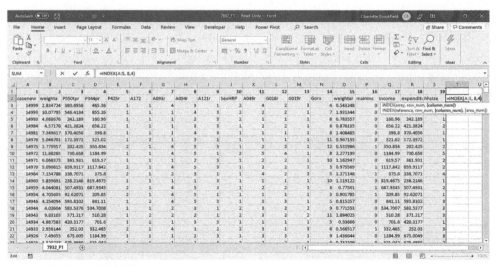

Figure 3.9   Index function in Excel

Alternatively, it may be beneficial to use the Match function. For instance, if you wanted to quickly identify the row which contained data relating to a specific respondent, you could use the Match function. In this instance, we would use the following formula: '=MATCH(Reference category, Column of Interest Reference, 0)'. By including '0' at the end of this formula we ensure that Excel only returns rows that provide an exact match to the reference category. In the example in Figure 3.10, the reference category is '14976'. Using the Match function, Excel searches the list of case number names in the column of interest (A) until it finds the case number '14976'. Excel then tells us which row contains all of respondent number 14976's data.

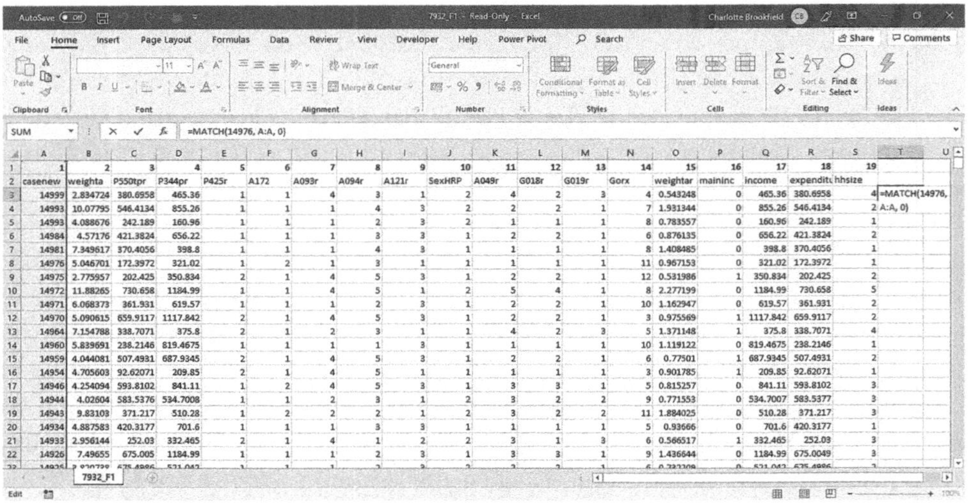

Figure 3.10   Match function (finding a row) in Excel

The Match function can also be used with column data. For example, it may be advantageous to identify which column contains the gross normal weekly household income variable (**P344pr**). In this example, the Match formula would state the following: '=MATCH(Reference category, Column Headings, 0)'. In Figure 3.11, the reference

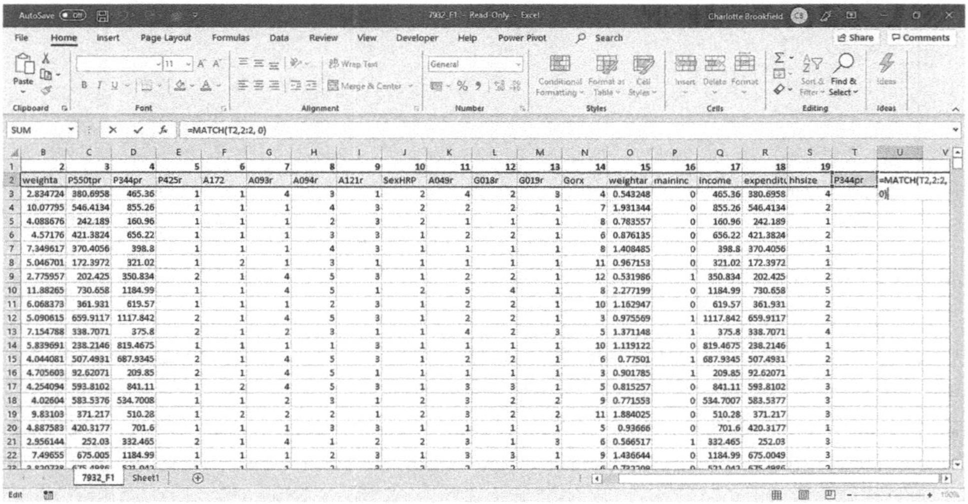

Figure 3.11   Match function (searching columns) in Excel

category is 'P344pr'. Note that, because this contains letters as well as numbers, you cannot simply type the variable name into the formula. Instead, the name is entered into the cell adjacent to the formula and this cell reference is then used in the formula. In this example, the column headings are in row 2, therefore '2:2' is entered into the formula. Excel searches the column headings until it finds one that matches the label 'P344pr'.

3.10 Concatenate

The concatenate function in Excel allows you to combine data from two or more cells. In the example in Tables 3.3 and 3.4, the concatenate function is used to combine first names and surnames.

Table 3.3 Concatenate function in Microsoft Excel

	A	B	C	D	E	F	G	H	I	J
1	**First**	**Last**	**Full**							
2	Sally	Smith	=concatenate (A2, B2)							
3	Bob	Wilson								
4	Rae	Harvey								
5										

Table 3.4 Concatenate function example in Microsoft Excel

	A	B	C	D	E	F	G	H	I	J
1	**First**	**Last**	**Full**							
2	Sally	Smith	SallySmith							
3	Bob	Wilson								
4	Rae	Harvey								
5										

By typing the concatenate formula the text appearing in two cells is put next to each other in a new cell. It is important to note that the concatenate function does not automatically insert a space between the data in the selected cells. In order to ensure that there is a space between data the formula needs to be adapted to the following: '=CONCATENATE(A2, " ", B2)'. Alternatively, a comma can be inserted between the two selected cells when the concatenate formula is adapted to the following: 'CONCATENATE(A2, ",", B2)'. Once data has been concatenated it can be easier to spot duplicates in a dataset.

3.11 Freezing Panes

Excel will allow users to freeze particular rows or columns while still scrolling through and viewing the rest of the spreadsheet. This can be particularly helpful when dealing with large datasets. This is because, in such situations, it can be hard to review the variable names as well as data at the same time. Freezing a row or column in Excel involves selecting the **View** option from the top toolbar. From here, you can select '**Freeze Panes**' and choose which part of your dataset you would like to freeze (see Figure 3.12).

View > Freeze Panes > Select area you want to freeze

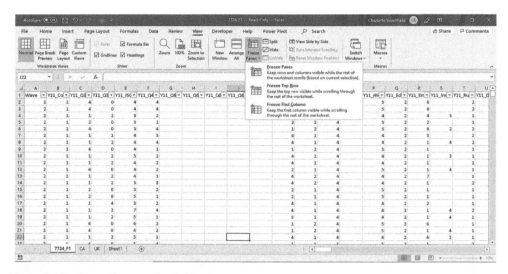

Figure 3.12   Freeze Panes option in Excel

You can choose to freeze just the top row of a worksheet or just the first column of a worksheet. These options mean that if you scroll down or across your worksheet respectively, you will continue to see the data or information in the first row or column. Instead, you can choose to freeze panes based on your current selection. In these scenarios, Excel will freeze all columns above, and all rows to the left, of the cell that you have selected.

3.12 Filtering Data

In some instances, you may not be interested in exploring all cases in a dataset. For example, you may want to analyse males and females separately and begin to make comparisons. In order to disaggregate data in this way, you can use the Excel Filter function. Under the '**Home**' tab, select '**Sort & Filter**' and then select '**Filter**'.

Home > Sort and Filter > Filter

A small downwards arrow will appear next to the column headings in the spreadsheet. By clicking the arrow, you can choose which data you want to display. Once selected, this will make the other options disappear and allow you to analyse selected cases only. Figure 3.13 shows the Filter option being used to show only data from UK respondents in the European Quality of Life Survey (2007). Country code 27 denotes UK participants in this example.

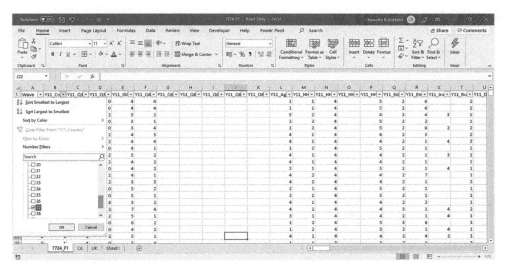

Figure 3.13   Using the Filter option in Excel to view data from UK respondents only

It is advisable to copy and paste (use the Paste Special function) the filtered data into a new worksheet prior to undertaking analysis. Excel will include data which is not visible and has been filtered out of the current view when undertaking statistical analysis. Therefore, it is important to copy the filtered data into a new worksheet before undertaking analysis. To turn the filter off, click the downwards arrow in the column heading again and click '**Select all**'.

3.13 Data Cleaning

When data is entered into a spreadsheet, it is possible that errors may occur. In an ideal world, it would be advantageous to have at least two people inputting the data simultaneously; however, this process is both costly and time-consuming. In order to avoid this but still ensure that data is 'clean' and accurate, it is advisable to run frequencies on each variable before undertaking any analysis. Running frequencies in this manner will help identify any spurious figures (see Sections 4.6 and 4.7).

3.13.1 Data (re)coding

In quantitative research, it is sometimes necessary to recode data. For example, if you have data on exact salaries (as a continuous scale), you may wish to recode this into bands representing low, medium and high earners. Alternatively, you may have data relating to a variable where a small minority of participants have given various different answers. In this situation, you may decide to recode all of these participants into an 'Other' category. In some circumstances, particularly when researchers have smaller sample sizes, researchers will recode responses to allow further analysis.

In Excel, the IF function allows you to recode data. In this example, the variable **'Gross normal weekly household income'** (P344pr) from the Living Costs and Food Survey (2013) has been recoded from a continuous scale to a categorical variable. The variable has been recoded into those households that had a gross normal weekly income above the average for the sample (**Greater than £620**) and those households that had a gross normal weekly income below or equal to the average for the sample (**Less than or equal to £620**). In this instance, you would use the IF function in Excel to recode the data. In the example, gross normal weekly household incomes greater than £620 are recoded as 1, while gross normal weekly household incomes equal to or less than £620 are recoded as 0. The IF formula should always be structured in the following way:

=IF(Logical test, Result if True, Result if False)

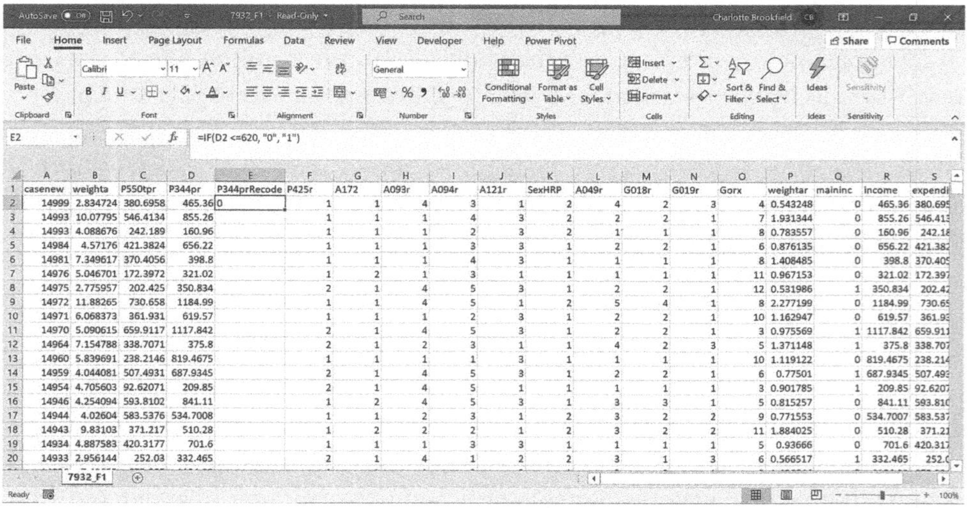

Figure 3.14   Using the IF function in Excel to recode the **P344pr** variable from the Living Costs and Food Survey (2013)

The logical test is a statement of what you wish to test – in this example whether or not the normal weekly household income is greater than £620. The result if true refers to the value that you want to appear if the logical test is true and the result if false refers to the value that you want to appear if the logical test is false.

To begin the recode, insert a new column in your spreadsheet (Figure 3.14). It is often easier to insert this new column adjacent to the one that you wish to recode.

The IF statement looks to see if the reference cell (in this instance, A2) meets the criteria given in the formula. In this example, when the condition is met, the cells will be coded as 0 and when it is not met they will be coded as 1 (i.e. they denote a gross normal weekly income which is greater than £620). Alternatively, you may wish cells to be recoded with textual labels. This can be done by replacing the '0' and '1' in the statement with words. For instance, we may choose instead to use the codes 'below' and 'above' in this example (see Figure 3.15).

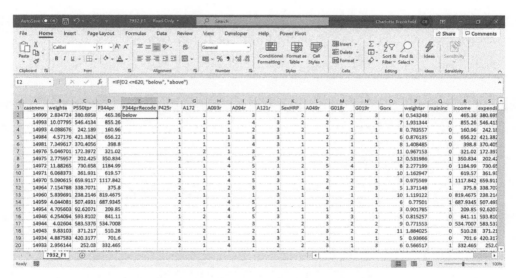

Figure 3.15 Using the IF function in Excel to recode the **P344pr** variable from the Living Costs and Food Survey (2013) into textual values

In some instances, it may be more appropriate to recode variables into more than two groups. For example, it may be more useful to split gross normal weekly income into three groups: low income (£400 or less); medium income (greater than £400, but less than £800); and high income (£800 or more). To do this, you would need to use multiple IF functions. This is demonstrated in Figure 3.16.

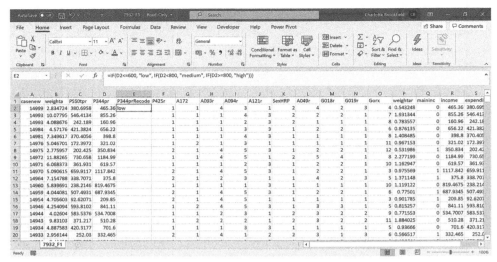

Figure 3.16 Using the IF function in Excel to recode the **P344pr** variable from the Living Costs and Food Survey (2013) into more than two categories

The operators in Table 3.5 can all be used with the IF function.

Table 3.5 Operators which can be used with the IF function

Operator	Meaning
=	Equal to
>	Greater than
<	Less than
>=	Greater than or Equal to
<=	Less than or Equal to
<>	Not Equal to

3.13.2 Finding missing data

While researchers should take steps prior to data collection to minimise the amount of missing data in a dataset, in reality it is sometimes the case that participants decide not to answer particular questions. For instance, participants may deem a question too intrusive or not understand how they are supposed to respond. An alternative situation which can result in missing data is when the researcher is unable to read the handwriting of a participant who has completed a survey by hand. It is important to consider whether the missing data in a dataset could introduce bias into a research project. For example, is it predominately female respondents who have not provided an answer to a particular question? If this is the case, it may potentially bias the analysis.

In some cases, researchers may have coded missing data during the process of inputting the data. Often, these researchers will code missing values as either –9, –99, or –999. In general, researchers code missing data with numbers that are not possible true figures. For instance, for a survey item measuring fruit and vegetable consumption, you may decide to record missing data as –99 as this is not a possible true response. It is important to look at any guidance that comes with existing data to ensure that you know if, and how, a researcher has coded data as missing. In some instances, researchers may provide different codes depending on whether the data is missing because a respondent refused to answer, or whether a respondent did not know the answer, or whether the question was not applicable to the respondent. For instance, the Quarterly Labour Force Survey (January–March 2015) contains reported missing values of –8 and –9. When exploring the variable **TOTHRS** (total hours worked in reference week), 8727 participants have the response –9, and 230 have the response –8. By looking at the supporting guidance that accompanies this dataset, it is possible to determine what these numbers denote. In this example, –9 was given when the question did not apply to a participant, while –8 was given when a participant did not give an answer. This shows that the majority of missing data associated with this variable is due to the question not being applicable to respondents as opposed to respondents not giving an answer. Once you know how missing data is coded within a dataset, you can use the Countif function in Excel to determine how much data is missing for each variable (see Section 4.7).

In other instances, you may get data that you wish to recode as missing. For example, when exploring the total number of hours worked in the reference work in the Labour Force Survey, there are some participants who report working over the UK legal limit of a 48-hour week average. While some professions are exempt from this rule, in this dataset there are participants who report working over double this number in the specified week. Because of this, we may infer that participants who reported particularly high numbers misinterpreted the question or calculated the number of hours that they worked incorrectly. Even if participants have correctly interpreted and answered the question, these outliers are likely to distort our analysis of the data. As a result, we may choose to classify all those who reported working over 60 hours in the reference week (or more than five 12-hour days) as missing from our dataset. Other examples may include where participants report eating in excess of 20 portions of fruit or vegetables a day or where they report body weights that seem implausible, such as less than 1kg.

The data validation tool in Excel can be used to identify and subsequently exclude missing data. For example, with the variable **TOTHRS** we could use the data validation tool to highlight all the cases in the data where participants reported working less than 0 or more than 60 hours per week. To run the data validation tool using a particular variable, begin by highlighting the column which contains the variable of interest. Then, select '**Data**' from the top toolbar and select the **Data Validation** option (Figure 3.17). This will open a new window. Ensure the '**Settings**' tab is visible in this new window.

Data > Data Validation > Settings

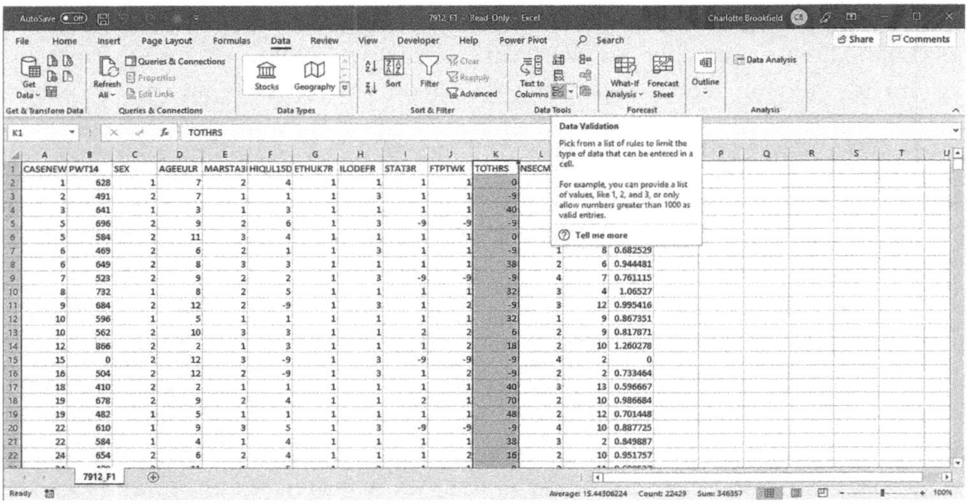

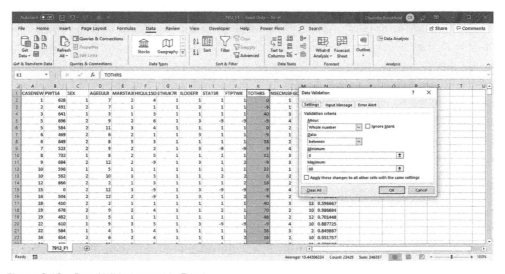

Figure 3.17 Opening the Data Validation tool in Excel

In the validation criteria, use the drop-down menu under the heading '**Allow**' to select '**Whole Number**'. Then, in turn, enter your minimum and maximum value for that variable. In this instance, our minimum value is 0 and our maximum value is 60. Click **OK** to proceed (Figure 3.18).

Figure 3.18 Data Validation tool in Excel

Allow: Whole Number

Minimum: 0

Maximum: 60

OK

Once you have entered these conditions in the Data Validation tool, you can ask Excel to circle invalid cases – or, in other words, to highlight the respondents who gave answers beyond the range of 0–60 hours per week. Again, this can be done by selecting '**Data**' from the top toolbar. You then need to select the drop-down menu next to the **Data Validation tool** and click '**Circle Invalid Data**'. This will prompt red ovals to appear around the cases which do not meet your chosen criteria.

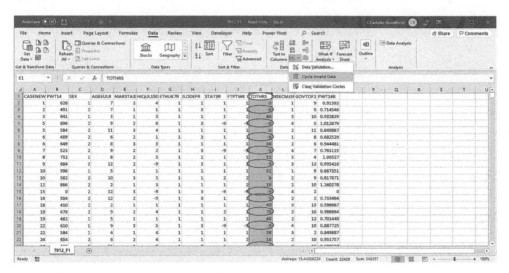

Figure 3.19   Circle Invalid Data function in Excel

3.13.3 Dealing with missing data

If you have identified missing data within a dataset, it is important to consider how you are going to deal with this data. As a researcher, it is necessary to decide whether to discount respondents with any missing data from all analysis, or whether it is more appropriate only to exclude respondents when they have missing data which relates to the key variables under investigation. The former option can severely limit the sample size of a dataset.

In Excel it is possible to filter the data so that only those respondents who have given valid responses are visible in the dataset and included in the analysis. The Advanced Filter option in Excel enables researchers to define the criteria by which they wish to filter their data. For instance, if we wish to exclude all those participants for whom the variable **TOTHRS** has missing data (-9 or -8 response) we could use the Advanced Filter function to create a copy of the dataset that excludes these respondents. To do this, it is necessary to create a list of criteria first. The criteria must have exactly the same column heading as the variable that you wish to filter by. Figure 3.20 shows an extract from the Quarterly Labour Force Survey (January–March 2015). Column P contains the filtering criteria – note that column P is given the same title as the variable name in column K. Cell P2 contains the criteria for this filter; in this instance the variable **TOTHRS** will be filtered to include only values greater than or equal to 0.

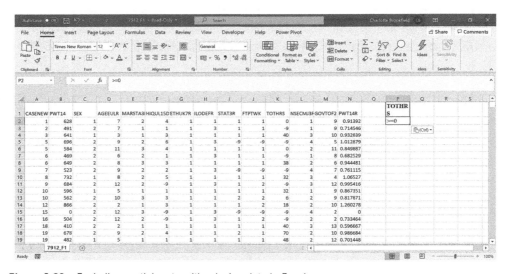

Figure 3.20 Excluding participants with missing data in Excel

To begin the filter, highlight the whole dataset (this can be done by holding down Ctrl and A at the same time) and select '**Data**' from the top toolbar. Under the '**Sort and Filter**' menu select '**Advanced**'. This will open a new window (Figure 3.21).

Data > Sort and Filter > Advanced

In this new window, select '**Copy to another loction**'. In '**List range**', highlight and select the data that you wish to filter. In '**Criteria range**', highlight and select the criteria that you have predefined (in this example cells P1 and P2). In '**Copy to**', select where you would like the new filtered dataset that does not include missing values to appear – this may be on a new worksheet in your workbook (see Figure 3.22).

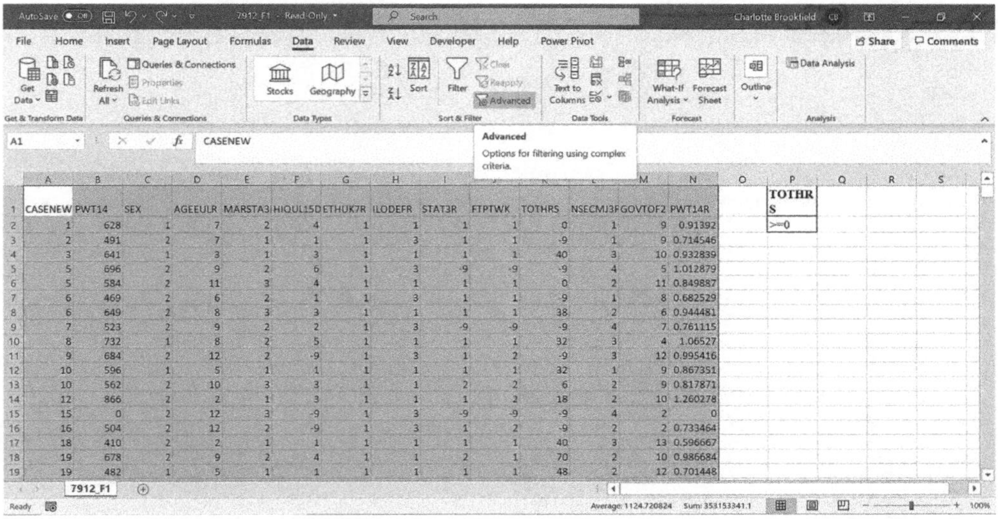

Figure 3.21   Selecting the Advanced Filter option in Excel

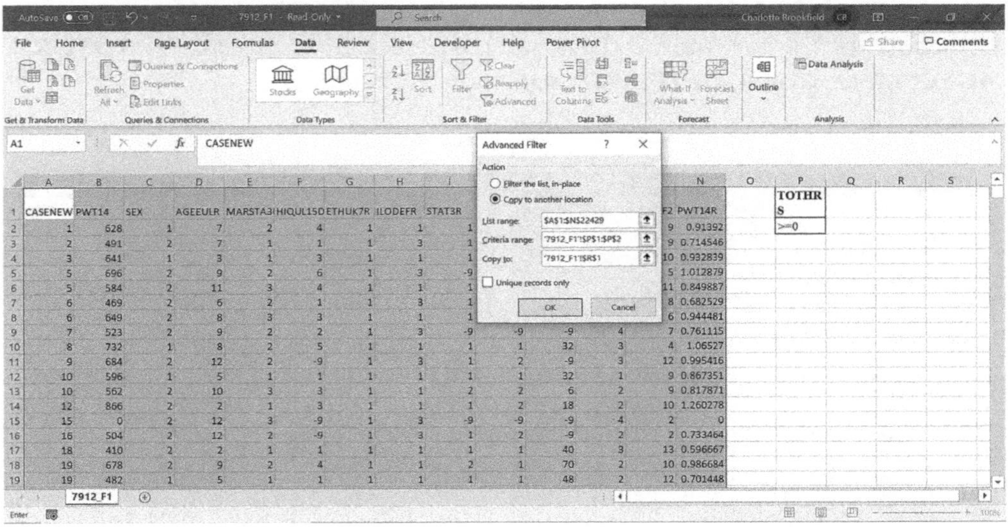

Figure 3.22   Using the Advanced Filter option in Excel

In addition to excluding those who reported negative values, if we wished to exclude those who had worked more than 60 hours, the criteria list would need to be updated. Figure 3.23 shows the updated criteria for this scenario.

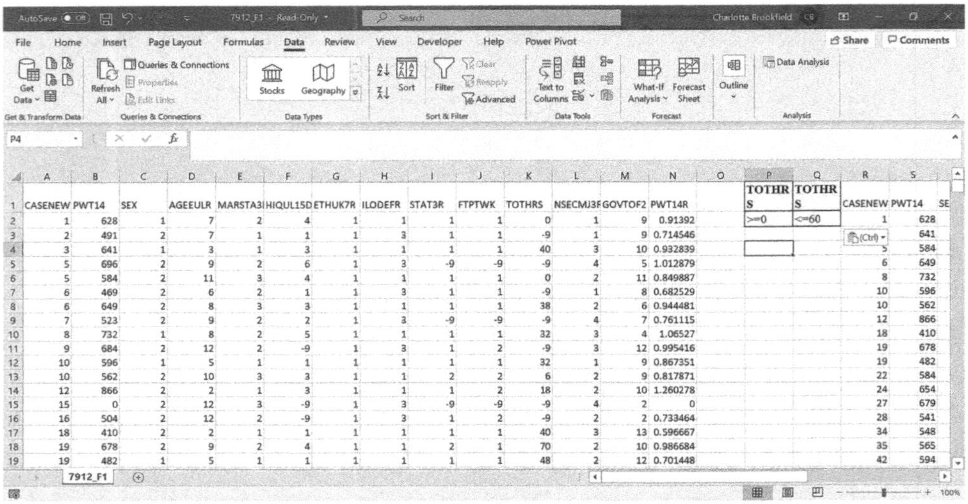

Figure 3.23 Excluding participants who reported working less than 0 or more than 60 hours a week

If there are multiple variables which you wish to filter by, these need to be added to your filter criteria. In Figure 3.24, the extract of data from the Quarterly Labour Force (January–March 2015) contains three variables. In this example, those for whom data is missing for the following variables were excluded from the dataset: **TOTHRS**, **AGEEULR** (age band), **HIQUL15D** (highest qualification).

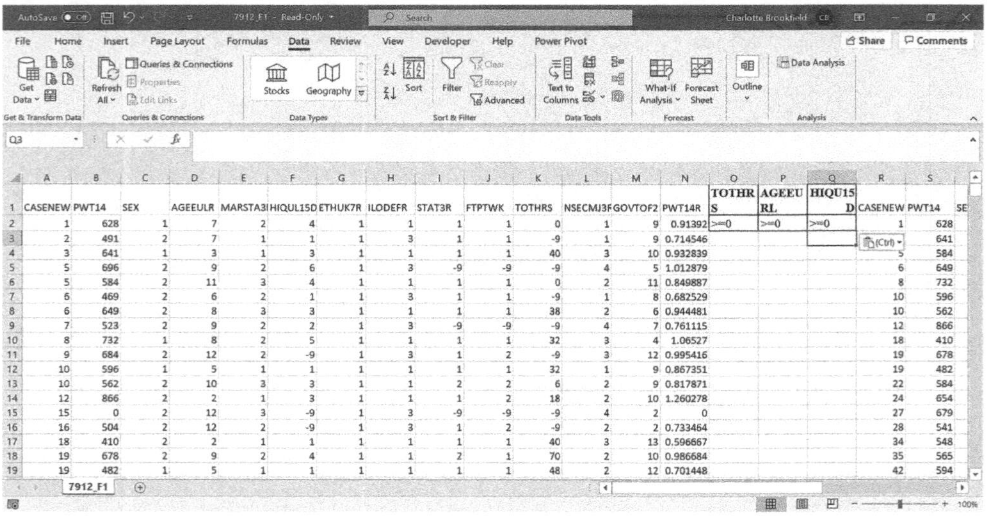

Figure 3.24 Excluding missing data across multiple variables

3.14 Assessing the Quality of Data

3.14.1 Validity

Validity refers to the extent to which a research instrument truly measures the concept that it was intended to measure. It is important that measures used in social science research are suitable to give the researcher adequate data in relation to the key issue under investigation. Often researchers will differentiate between different types of validity. These include face validity, internal validity, external validity and ecological validity.

Face Validity

It is crucial when designing new research instruments to ensure that they are able to demonstrate face validity – that is, they at least appear to measure the concepts or phenomena that they were intended to. It can be useful to get other people (outsiders from the research) to help assess the face validity of new measures designed for a specific research project.

Internal Validity

Internal validity refers to the extent to which researchers can be confident that it is a change in their independent variable that is causing a resultant change in their dependent variable. In reality, there are often other confounding variables that may also be attributable for the change seen in the dependent variable. It is the responsibility of the researcher to pre-empt these confounding variables and to control for them. For instance, if the researcher was exploring the relationship between how much exercise students reported doing that day and current hunger levels, it may also be important to ask the students to report when they last ate and what they ate.

External Validity

If the findings of a study are externally valid, it means that they can be generalised beyond the sample to the wider population. In quantitative research, researchers often strive to obtain samples that are representative of the wider population. By doing this, it is easier for the researchers to assert external validity and generalise the findings of their study beyond their sample.

Ecological Validity

Ecological validity refers to the extent to which the findings of a study reflect the real-world situation and context. It is important to consider the extent to which the findings of a social science study hold true in people's natural, everyday settings. It may be that the unnaturalness of the research process, or the setting in which the research is undertaken, jeopardises the ecological validity of a study.

3.14.2 Reliability

Reliability refers to consistency. Specifically, it is an indication of how consistent different measures are at understanding and measuring the same thing. In quantitative research, it is commonplace to have multiple indicators that attempt to measure or tap into the same underlying construct or phenomenon. This is known as 'internal reliability'. Internal reliability is measured by calculating a Cronbach's alpha score on a set, or series of survey Likert-scale questions, that are designed to measure the same thing. Cronbach's alpha scores vary between 1 (indicating perfect internal reliability) and 0 (indicating no internal reliability). As a rule of thumb, a score equal to or greater than 0.8 is deemed to denote a satisfactory level of internal reliability. However, Pallant (2007) cautions that where survey questions use short scales, the threshold for Cronbach's alpha may need to be lowered.

Other types of reliability referred to in social science research include 'stability'. Stable measures in quantitative research are those that yield the same results from a sample of respondents at different time points. This means that if we were to test a series of questions on a group of participants and then later re-administer the same questions to the same group, we could expect very little fluctuation or difference in how they would respond between the two time points.

Meanwhile, 'inter-observer' or 'inter-judge reliability' is concerned with the consistency with which two or more people who are involved with the research observe and record the same thing. This can be particularly important in projects where multiple researchers are coding data, for instance when undertaking content analysis. In these circumstances, it is important to ensure that there is a high level of inter-observer reliability and that the different researchers are using the same approach and criteria to code the data.

Remember Box 3.1

What Is the Difference between Validity and Reliability?

Validity: Concerned with how accurately survey questions and tools measure an underlying construct or phenomenon.

Reliability: Concerned with the consistency with which survey questions and tools tap into an underlying construct or phenomenon. Internal reliability can be determined using Cronbach's alpha scores.

A survey item can be reliable but not valid. For instance, you may record the temperature using the same faulty thermometer every day – as long as the thermometer was consistently faulty, your results would be reliable but would not be valid.

3.14.3 Calculating Cronbach's alpha in Excel

It is possible to calculate Cronbach's alpha scores using Excel. The simplest way to do this is to use the Anova Two-Factor Without Replication data analysis tool in Excel. In this example, data from the *Public Attitudes to Animal Research Survey, 2016* has been used. In this survey, there are 10 questions relating to views on the acceptability of animal research. These variables are: **3a** (I can accept the use of animals in research as long as it is for medical research purposes and there is no alternative), **3b** (There needs to be more work done into alternatives to using animals in scientific research), **3c** (I can accept the use of animals in scientific research as long as there is no unnecessary suffering to the animals), **3d** (Animals should not be used in any scientific research because of the importance I place on animal welfare), **3e** (It does not bother me if animals are used in scientific research), **3f** (The use of animals for medical research should only be conducted for life-threatening

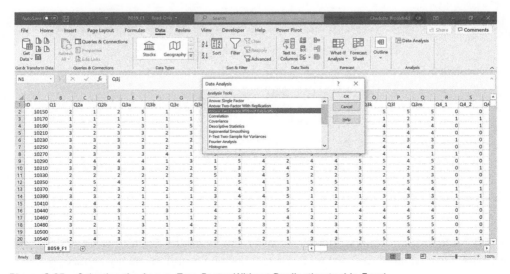

Figure 3.25 Selecting the Anova: Two-Factor Without Replication tool in Excel

or debilitating diseases), **3g** (The UK government should ban the use of animals for any form of research), **3h** (Acceptable to use animals in research to help our understanding of the human body, where there is no alternative), **3i** (Acceptable to use animals in research to help our understanding of animal health, where there is no alternative) **3j** (Acceptable to use animals for all types of research where there is no alternative). To deduce whether all of these variables truly tap into the same underlying construct 'acceptability of animal research', a Cronbach's alpha score needs to be calculated. To do this in Excel, select '**Data**' from the top menu toolbar. Then select '**Data Analysis**'. (If the Data Analysis option does not appear, follow the instructions in Section 3.5.1 to install the Analysis ToolPak). This will open a new window, where you need to select '**Anova: Two-Factor Without Replication**' (Figure 3.25).

Data > Data Analysis >Anova: Two-Factor Without Replication

For '**Input Range**' select the data that you wish to analyse (Figure 3.26). If you have included the variable names in your selection, make sure that you tick the '**Labels**' box. Under '**Output Options**' select where you would like the results of the analysis to appear. Then select **OK**. This will create output that you will need to use to calculate the Cronbach's alpha score.

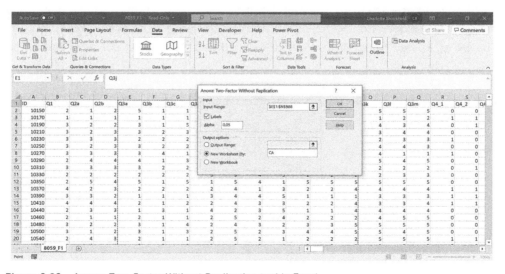

Figure 3.26   Anova: Two-Factor Without Replication tool in Excel

To calculate the Cronbach's alpha score, you need to use the mean squared errors value and the mean squared rows value. These can both be found in the last table of output. Note that Excel uses *MS* to denote mean squared (Figure 3.27).

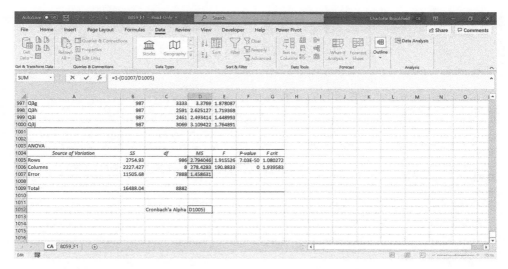

Figure 3.27 Excel output needed to calculate the Cronbach's alpha score

In a new cell, type the following: '1-(Cell reference for MS Error/Cell reference for MS Row)'.

The resultant figure will be the Cronbach's alpha score. In this example, the MS Error is 2.79 and the MS Row is 1.46. This results in a final Cronbach's alpha score of 0.48.

Further Reading

Burrows, R. and Savage, M. 2014. After the Crisis? Big Data and the Methodological Challenges of Empirical Sociology. *Big Data and Society* 1(1), pp. 1–6.

Carmines, E.G. and Zeller, R.A. 1980. *Quantitative Applications in the Social Sciences: Reliability and Validity Assessment*. London: Sage.

Savage, M. and Burrows, R. 2007. The Coming Crisis of Empirical Sociology. *Sociology* 41(5), pp. 885–899.

UK Data Service. *Top Ten Tips to Citing Data*. Available at: https://www.ukdataservice. ac.uk/media/622247/toptentips.pdf [Accessed 30 July 2019].

Skills Checklist for Chapter 3

Use the checklist provided to track your learning and to highlight areas where you may need to do some additional reading.

	I can do this confidently	I could do this if I had a little more practice	I need more help with this
Reference a dataset			

(Continued)

	I can do this confidently	I could do this if I had a little more practice	I need more help with this
Code data			
Install the Analysis ToolPak in Microsoft Excel			
Use the Vlookup and Hlookup functions in Microsoft Excel			
Use the Index and Match functions in Microsoft Excel			
Use the Concatenate function in Microsoft Excel			
Filter data using Microsoft Excel			
Identify missing data using Microsoft Excel			
Remove missing data from a dataset using Microsoft Excel			
Assess whether data is valid			
Assess whether data is reliable			
Calculate Cronbach's alpha in Microsoft Excel			

---(**Ideas for Teachers/Instructors**)---------------------

Data Everywhere

Get your students to list all the instances where their data has been collected in the past 24–48 hours. Encourage them to think about the type of data that they routinely share with different companies and organisations within their everyday lives. Ask them to think about what happens with this data and how it is used.

Validity and Reliability (in Pie Making)

Use Nassif and Khalil's (2006) 'Pie metaphor' to help teach the concepts of validity and reliability:

Nassif, N. and Khalil, Y. 2006. Making a Pie as a Metaphor for Teaching Scale Validity and Reliability. *American Journal of Evaluation* 27(3), pp. 393–398.

4

GETTING FAMILIAR WITH YOUR DATA

Understanding and describing data using Microsoft Excel

Colour Code for Chapter:
Green
Study Skills:
Analysing and interpreting data
Research Methods Skills:
Levels of data, Measures of central tendency, Measures of spread, Normality
Microsoft Excel Skills:
Summary Statistics, Countif, Normality Checks (including creating a histogram)
Datasets Used in This Chapter:
Living Costs and Food Survey, 2013: Unrestricted Access Teaching Dataset
Public Attitudes to Animal Research Survey, 2016
Quarterly Labour Force Survey Household Dataset, January–March, 2015

Visit **https://study.sagepub.com/brookfield** to download the datasets used in this chapter.

Chapter Outline

In this chapter you will learn how to differentiate between different levels of data in a dataset. In the social sciences, we mostly work with categorical data, but in some instances we also need to be able to analyse continuous level data. It is important to be able to determine what level of data each variable in a dataset contains. This is because the data level often dictates which statistical test is most appropriate to analyse your data. This chapter will also describe some initial steps that you can take when analysing data in order to get a greater familiarity with the dataset and the possible responses.

4.1 Introduction

When analysing quantitative data for a research project, researchers often begin with univariate analysis. Univariate analysis refers to situations where the researcher analyses only one variable at a time. Such analysis allows the researcher to understand how participants have responded to each survey item in a questionnaire. In some cases, researchers will undertake some preliminary univariate analysis to allow them to explore their data and get a 'feel' for it before potentially recoding it or recording responses as missing (see Sections 3.14.2 and 3.14.3). Univariate analysis involves reporting measures of central tendency and measures of spread. Each of these will be discussed in this chapter. The level of data and the results of univariate analysis can dictate subsequent, more complex analysis, therefore it is a vital first step in the data analysis process. Another part of univariate analysis can be creating visual representations of the variables under exploration. Chapter 9 describes the appropriate visual representation for categorical variables and provides guidance on how to produce them in Excel. By the end of this chapter, you will be able to use Excel to get an initial 'feel' for your data.

4.2 Levels of Data

At the start of a project, it is important to identify the type of data that is in a dataset. The level of the data that is available will dictate the statistical analysis that you can carry out later in your project.

Broadly, data can be split into two categories: categorical data and continuous data (see Table 4.1). Categorical data can be further divided into ordinal data and nominal data. Ordinal data refers to data which has a label or textual response that falls into some sort of hierarchy. For instance, highest educational qualification is an example of an ordinal variable. People may report that their highest-level qualifications are GSCEs (or equivalent), others may say A levels (or equivalent) and others may report having a degree-level qualification. These responses can be ordered from the qualification which is deemed the lowest to the qualification which is deemed the highest. Likert scales (scales ranging from strongly agree to strongly disagree, or very important to very unimportant) are another example of ordinal data. Nominal data refers to data which also has a label or textual value; however, it does not have an order. For instance, gender and favourite colour are all examples of nominal data. While some may try to order response categories for nominal variables, this will be based on their own subjective judgements, while ordinal variables are inherently ordered. Continuous level data can also be split into two groups. These are known as interval level data and ratio data. Interval level data always has a numerical value and the difference between the values is standardised and meaningful. Examples of interval data include bank balance and temperature. Similarly, ratio data also has numerical values with differences that are standardised and meaningful; however, ratio data has a true zero value. This means that ratio data cannot have minus values. Examples of ratio data include height, household income, number of children in a household. It is not possible to be minus 143cm tall; therefore the scale has a true zero value.

Table 4.1 Levels of data

Level of Data		Definition	Example
Categorical Variables	Nominal	Categorical data that has no hierarchy	Hair colour, favourite food, gender, ethnicity
	Ordinal	Categorical data that has a hierarchy	Level of education, Likert scale: strongly agree–strongly disagree
Continuous Variables	Interval	Numerical data on a scale Can have negative values	Bank balance, temperature
	Ratio	Numerical data on a scale There is an absolute zero value	Height, weight, salary

In general, continuous-level data is considered to be of the highest quality. This is because this data is more detailed and enables us to engage with a greater variety of statistical tests. However, in social science research there tends to be more categorical data and much less continuous-level data.

— Remember Box 4.1—

What are nominal-, ordinal- and continuous-level variables?

Nominal variables: Categorical variables where the response categories are not ordered. Response categories are arbitrary and have no value (e.g. ethnicity, gender, political party affiliation).

(Continued)

Ordinal variables: Categorical variables where the response categories have an inherent order. Response categories fall into a hierarchy (e.g. strongly agree–strongly disagree, level of education).

Continuous variables: Variables that have a numeric response. The distance between each response value is the same and constant (e.g. the distance between 1 and 2 is the same as the distance between 45 and 46). Continuous variables are more uncommon in social science research. Examples include: height, number of people in household, number of cars owned per household, number of times a person has been a victim of crime.

4.3 Measures of Central Tendency

When analysing quantitative data, researchers often begin by reporting measures of central tendency for key variables of interest in the dataset. These measures give the reader a sense of what a typical person or case in the study sample is like. The measures that are often reported are the mean, median and mode. The measure(s) that you report for any given variable are determined by the level of data.

For continuous-level data, all three measures of central tendency can be calculated and reported (mean, median and mode). For ordinal-level data, it is not possible to calculate the mean and therefore it is only necessary to report the median and the mode. For nominal-level data, it is only possible to calculate and report the mode.

The mode refers to the value which occurs most or is most commonly found in the dataset. For some variables, there may be more than one mode. For instance, the dataset may contain equal numbers of people who reported pizza as their favourite food as the number who reported burgers as their favourite food. The median value is either the middle value, or, if there are an even number of values, the value half-way between the middle two values, once the data has been sorted from lowest to highest. The mean refers to the arithmetic average. This is calculated by adding all the values and dividing the total by the number of respondents who have provided data. The mean utilises all the data in the sample, the disadvantage being that the value can be influenced by outliers in the sample.

Remember Box 4.2

When and how do you calculate the mean, median and mode?

Mean: The arithmetic average (add up all the values and divide by the total number of responses). Calculate for continuous data only.

Median: The middle value (order values from smallest to largest and find the middle value). Calculate for continuous and ordinal data.

Mode: The most occurring value (see which response is stated most frequently). Calculate for continuous, ordinal and nominal data.

4.4 Measures of Spread

A further way of describing key variables of interest is by reporting measures of spread. This is particularly helpful because it can tell you the range of values for a given variable and can help you determine whether measures of central tendency may be influenced by extreme outliers in the dataset (it can also help reveal whether negative values have been used to code missing data in a dataset; see Section 3.14.2). The range is the difference between the highest and the lowest value of a variable in a dataset. This can only be reported for continuous level variables and is calculated by subtracting the minimum value for a variable from the maximum value for the same variable. Another measure of spread that is frequently reported for continuous level variables is the standard deviation. The standard deviation refers to the spread of the data from the mean. When the standard deviation is large it suggests that the mean is not a very good predictor of the average, whereas when the standard deviation is small it is likely that the mean is fairly representative of a typical response.

Remember Box 4.3

What are the range and standard deviation and when do I calculate them?

Range: The difference between the smallest and largest value. Calculate for continuous level variables only.

Standard deviation: How far away the values are from the mean. A small standard deviation suggests that the data is clustered around the mean value and therefore the mean is a good indicator of a typical case in the data. A large standard deviation suggests that the data is not concentrated around the mean value and therefore the mean may not be a good indicator of a typical case in the data. In this situation, it is possible that the large spread of values in your data will introduce outliers into your analysis. Calculate for continuous level variables only.

4.5 Distribution of Data

For continuous level variables, further consideration of the distribution of the data is often needed. Specifically, it is good practice to see whether the variable of interest is normally distributed. Normally distributed data adopts a bell curve shape when graphed as a histogram. For normally distributed data, it is expected that 68% of the data will fall within one standard deviation either side of the mean value, 95% of the data will fall within two standard deviations either side of the mean value and 99.7% of data will fall within three standard deviations either side of the mean value. If data is normally distributed, the continuous variable will often have a very similar value for the mean, median and mode. Height, birth weight and population IQ are all examples of normally distributed variables that we encounter every day.

Another way to assess whether a continuous level variable is normally distributed is by plotting the data on a histogram and investigating skew and kurtosis. Skew refers to symmetry; if skewness is equal to 0 it suggests that the histogram displaying the variable of interest is symmetrical. If the histogram is not symmetrical and instead has a long 'tail' on the right and is peaked on the left, the data for that variable is positively skewed. Alternatively, if the histogram appears to have a long 'tail' on the left and is peaked on the right, the data for the variable is negatively skewed (see Figure 4.1).

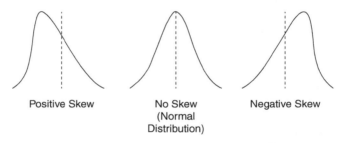

Positive Skew   No Skew   Negative Skew
                 (Normal
                 Distribution)

Figure 4.1 Histograms showing skew

Kurtosis measures the size of the 'tails' on a histogram. When each vertical bar on a histogram is fairly equal and the tails on the graph are short, the distribution can be described as platykurtic. In these instances, the kurtosis value is likely to be less than 2.

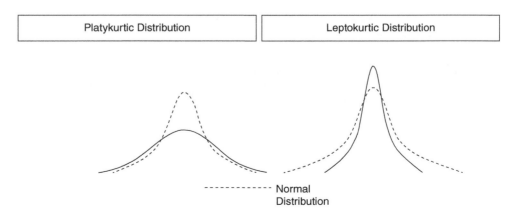

Figure 4.2 Histograms showing kurtosis

A histogram which has long tails and is very peaked shows a leptokurtic distribution. In these instances, the kurtosis value is likely to be greater than 2 (Figure 4.2). As well as being able to produce histograms, Excel provides you with skew and kurtosis values. If the skew and kurtosis values for a variable fall between −2 and +2, it may suggest that the data is normally distributed.

It is important to know whether a variable is normally distributed as this often determines which analysis is most appropriate. Many of the statistical tests discussed in this book and elsewhere rely on the assumption of normality; therefore, if your variable is not normally distributed, you risk violating these assumptions. Fortunately, a number of equivalent tests have been created for data which is not normally distributed (these will be explored further in later chapters).

4.6 Descriptive Statistics in Excel

Excel allows you to calculate descriptive statistics and frequencies for chosen variables quickly and easily. Once the **Analysis ToolPak** is installed (see Section 3.5.1), you can calculate descriptive statistics including measures of central tendency and measures of spread by selecting the following (Figure 4.3):

DATA > Data Analysis > Descriptive Statistics > OK

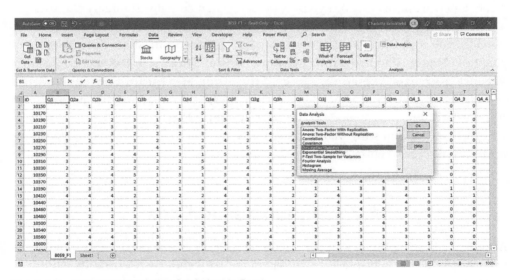

Figure 4.3 Running '**Descriptive Statistics**' in Excel

You then need to select the column that contains the variable of interest and choose where you would like the output to be presented. Output can be presented in a specific area in the present worksheet, on a new worksheet or in a new workbook (a new and separate document). '**Summary statistics**' needs to be checked and, if applicable, select '**Labels in first row**'. Finally, click **OK** to see the relevant output. Figure 4.4 shows this process.

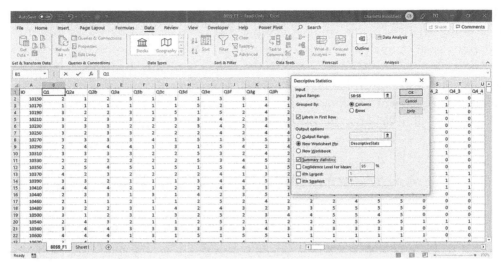

Figure 4.4 'Descriptive Statistics' window in Excel

Repeat the process for every variable of interest in the dataset. It may be helpful to create a new worksheet within your workbook which contains summary statistics for all key variables that have been identified. The Descriptive Statistics function in Excel provides you with the following key information (items in **bold** are discussed in this chapter): **Mean**, Standard Error, **Median**, **Mode**, **Standard Deviation**, Sample Variance, **Kurtosis**, **Skewness**, **Range**, **Minimum**, **Maximum**, Sum and **Count**.

Note, as discussed in Chapter 3 (see Section 3.13), it is important to copy and paste filtered data into a new worksheet before running descriptive statistics, otherwise Excel will include missing values (potentially negative numbers) when calculating measures of spread, central tendency and distribution.

4.7 Frequencies in Excel

As well as reporting the number of respondents for each variable, for categorical variables it can also be advantageous to report the frequency of respondents who gave specific answers. This gives an insight into the distribution of the data across respondents. This can be calculated in Excel using the Countif function. For instance, in the example shown here, the Countif function is used to see how survey participants responded to the question 'How well informed do you feel about the use of animals in scientific research in the UK?' in the *Public Attitudes to Animal Research Survey, 2016.*

For this question, respondents could report any of the following responses: **1** (Very well informed), **2** (Fairly well informed), **3** (Not very well informed), **4** (Not at all informed), **5** (Don't know) or **6** (None of these). The Countif function shows the frequency with which each response option (1, 2, 3, 4, 5 or 6) was reported (Figure 4.5).

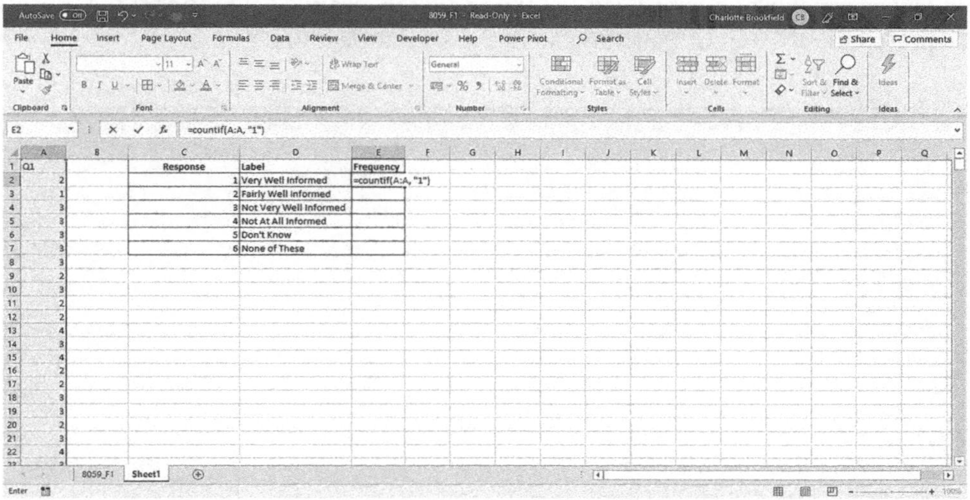

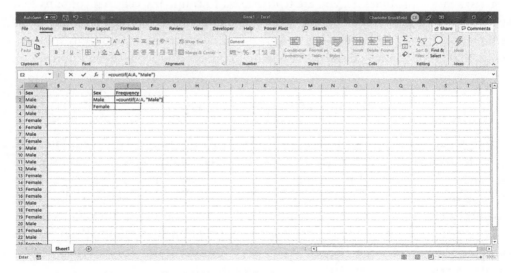

Figure 4.5 Countif function in Excel

The Countif function can also be used with textual data: for example, if the dataset recorded respondents as either male or female. You could use the Countif function with these textual labels (see example in Figure 4.6).

Figure 4.6 Countif function in Excel (with textual data)

The Countif function is case sensitive so it is important to enter the function carefully. Occasionally, when data has been inputted, there may be a space after the text. In these situations, the Countif function will not count the data. In order to remove the space and keep the text only, in a new column use the Trim function. To use the Trim function, enter the formula '=TRIM()'. In the brackets insert the coordinates of the first cell for the variable of interest; you can then drag the formula down so that the process is repeated for all cases of that variable in the spreadsheet (see Figure 4.7).

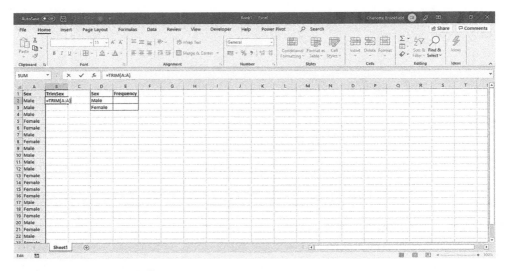

Figure 4.7 Trim function in Excel

In addition, sometimes you may use the =COUNTIF("**") function. By inserting the asterisks inside the brackets, you are telling Excel to count any cell that contains that particular word/part of a word. For example, you may want to count all participants who reported any of the following words: environment, environmental, environmentally. To do this, you would use the following formula: '=COUNTIF("*environment*")'.

4.8 Conditional Formatting

Conditional formatting can be used to colour-code cells in a dataset in a meaningful way. This can help a researcher get an initial 'feel' for the data. For instance, if a researcher was interested in looking at school-level data and wanted to see which schools in their local area had more than 50% of children receiving free school meals, then they may use conditional formatting as a starting point in their exploration.

To enable conditional formatting, begin by highlighting the data that you wish to format. Then, under the '**Home**' tab, select '**Conditional Formatting**'. Select '**Color Scales**' and '**More Rules**' (see Figure 4.8).

Home > Conditional Formatting > Color Scales > More Rules

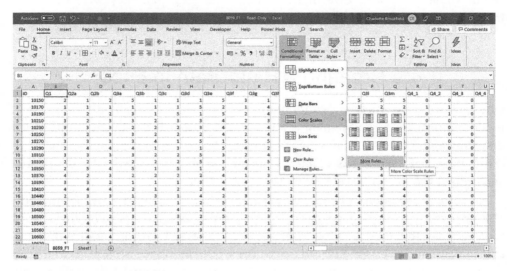

Figure 4.8 'Conditional Formatting' in Excel

This will open a new dialog box which will allow you to select which colours will appear when particular values are present. Once you are happy with your selection, click **OK**. Your cells should now change colour according to the rule that you have inputted. In this example, the question 'How well informed do you feel about the use of animals in scientific research in the UK?' from the *Public Attitudes to Animal Research Survey, 2016* has had conditional formatting applied. Here, the cells of respondents

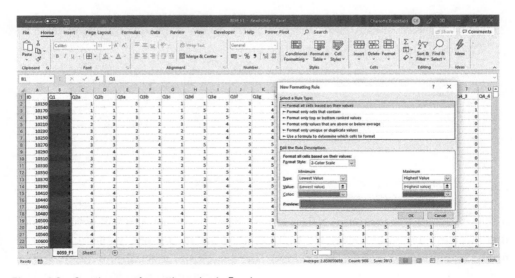

Figure 4.9 Creating new formatting rules in Excel

who reported low scores (indicating that they were very well informed) appear in one colour while those who gave higher scores (indicating that they were not at all informed) appear in another (see Figure 4.9).

4.9 Creating a Histogram in Excel

One way to decide whether a continuous level variable is normally distributed is to produce a histogram. A histogram is a graph that depicts the frequency with which different responses were reported and, in turn, allows you to explore the 'shape' or distribution that the data has adopted. Guidance on how to create graphs for nominal and ordinal variables in Excel is provided in Chapter 9.

To create a histogram in Excel, you need to begin by creating a table of bin limits. This table tells you the frequency with which values within fixed ranges were reported for a variable. To choose your bin size, you need to begin by reporting the minimum and maximum values for the variable under exploration (see Section 4.6). In this instance, we are looking at the variable **p344pr** (Gross normal household weekly income) from the Living Costs and Food Survey (2013). The minimum value for this variable is £0 and the maximum is £1184.99 (see Figure 4.10).

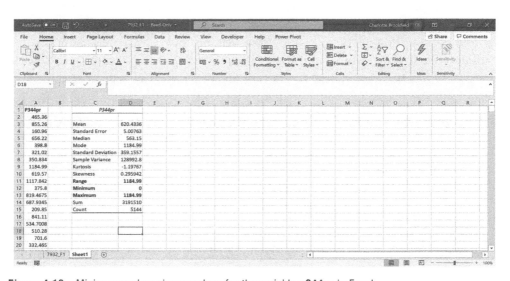

Figure 4.10   Minimum and maximum values for the variable **p344pr** in Excel

If the minimum and maximum values are not whole numbers, you will need to round them. For the minimum value, always round down to the nearest whole number, and for the maximum value, always round up to the nearest whole number. In this example, it is only the maximum value that needs rounding, and this is rounded up to £1185.

Once you have identified the minimum and maximum number, you need to determine the number of bins that you want. The greater the number of observations in your dataset, the greater the number of bins you will choose. The number of observations can be determined by looking at the 'Count' in the descriptive statistics table. In the example shown in Figure 4.10, 5144 people responded to the survey question and 10 bins have been chosen.

Following this, you need to divide the range by the chosen number of bins. In this example, it would be:

1184.99/10=118.499

This value gives you the size of your bins. For example, in this instance the first bin would range from £0 to £118.50. The upper limit for the next bin would be £237 (118.50 + 118.50). This process is repeated until you reach the maximum value – in this case, £1184.99. Rather than type the formula multiple times, it is possible to use the F4 lock function or to insert '$' signs around the reference cell which contains the bin size – in this example, cell G2 (see Figure 4.11).

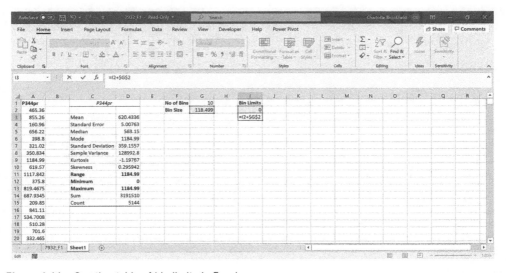

Figure 4.11 Creating table of bin limits in Excel

Alternatively, it is possible to calculate the number of bins and, in turn, the size of the bins using Sturge's rule. This rule is:

Number of bins = 1 + 3.322 log(n)

where n is equal to the number of observations

Continuing to use the **p344pr** variable (Gross normal average weekly household income), Sturge'srule would suggest that we need 14 bins, for example:

Number of bins = 1 + 3.322 log(5144) = 13.328 941

Sturge's rule can be calculated using Excel. In a cell, type the following, where n is equal to the number of observations in your sample:

=1+(3.32*LOG10(n))

Once you have identified the number of bins using Sturge's rule, you can calculate the size of the bins using the same method described above.

Once the bin limits table is complete, a graph of the data needs to be produced to see if it adopts a normal distribution. To create a histogram (Figure 4.12), you need to complete the following steps:

DATA > Data Analysis > Histograms > OK

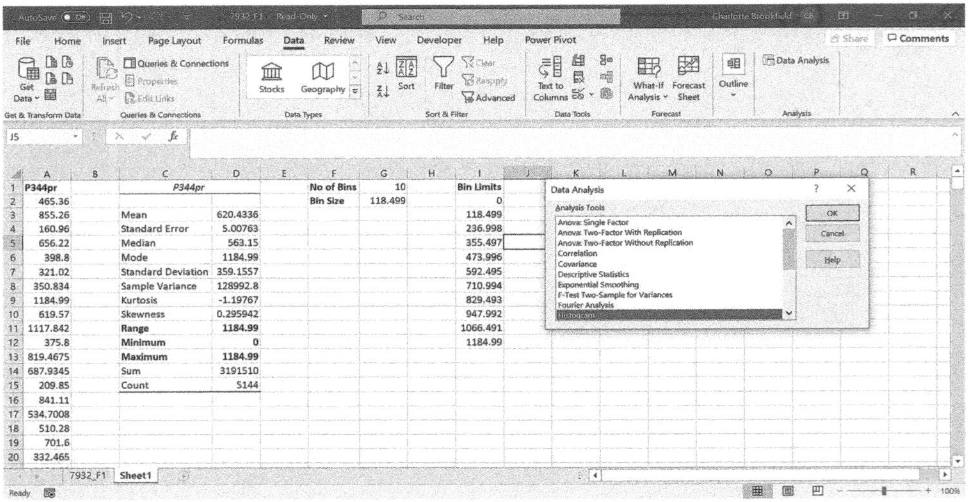

Figure 4.12 Inserting a histogram in Excel

In the new window, you will be prompted to enter the '**Input Range**' and the '**Bin Range**' (see Figure 4.13). '**Input Range**' refers to your variable of interest. Highlight the cells containing data relating to the variable which you wish to explore and enter this in the 'Input Range' box. In the 'Bin Range' box enter the cells in the 'Bin Limits' table. If applicable, check the box to indicate that you have highlighted the variable labels or names. After this, you need to tell Excel where you would like the output to appear. Finally, in order to produce a histogram, the '**Chart Output**' option must be selected. Once you click **OK** the histogram will be produced.

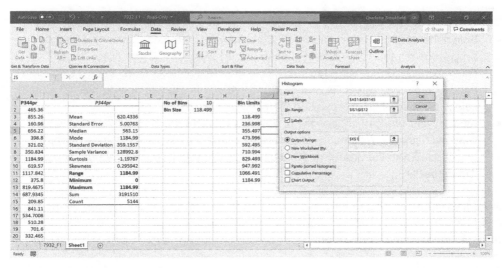

Figure 4.13 Creating a histogram in Excel

The frequency table and histogram show you the distribution of responses.

Activity

Calculate Summary Statistics

1. Download the Quarterly Labour Force Survey (January–March, 2015) Unrestricted Access Teaching Dataset

The Labour Force Survey is the largest, regular social survey in the UK. It primarily explores the themes of employability and economic activity; however, the survey also contains demographic data and questions on training and education. Working with the Teaching Dataset can be easier, because it contains fewer cases and fewer variables. In this instance, the Labour Force Teaching Data set only contains 30% of the sample that participated in the study.

To access the Quarterly Labour Force Survey (January–March 2015) Teaching Data set, you need to visit the UK Data Service website using the address below:

www.ukdataservice.ac.uk

Once the webpage has loaded, select '**Get Data**' and, in the search box, type the following:

quarterly labour force survey unrestricted access teaching dataset 2015

(Continued)

Select the January–March 2015 dataset. In the new window, select the purple box labelled '**Access Data**'. There are two ways to download the data. The first is by downloading the TAB file and the second is by accessing the data online. Both approaches are described here.

- Select the option to download the TAB file format of the data. Save the TAB data file on your computer. Then, open Excel and select '**File**' and '**Open**'. Browse for the TAB file, making sure that '**All Files**' are visible (the default is 'All Excel Files'). Once you have located the correct file, select '**Open**'. After this a series of windows will appear; select '**Next**' to each of these and then choose '**Finish**'.
- Alternatively, you can choose the option '**Access Online**'. This will open a new window. Click the 'Download' button, towards the right in the top toolbar (floppy disc icon). From the drop-down menu, select '**Comma Separated Value**' and click '**Download**'.

In addition to downloading the data, it is often helpful to download the supporting documents for the dataset. These documents include information on how the variables in the dataset are measured and coded.

2. Exclude missing cases

Check the supporting documentation for the dataset to see how missing data is coded for each of the variables. Using the instructions in Section 3.14.3, exclude these values.

3. Calculate summary statistics for each variable

Using Table 4.2, identify those variables for which it is appropriate to calculate the mean, median and/or mode (tick in the box). Also identify whether it is appropriate to report the range, standard deviation, skew and kurtosis values for each the variable. Note that weighting variables are not used in this task.

Table 4.2 Identifying what descriptive statistics to report

Variable Name	Variable Label	Mean	Median	Mode	Range	Standard Deviation	Skew	Kurtosis
SEX	Respondent's gender							
AGEEULR	Age bands in 5-year intervals							
MARSTA3AR	Marital status							
HIQUL15D	Highest qualification							
ETHUK7R	Ethnicity							
ILODEFR	Economic activity							

Variable Name	Variable Label	Mean	Median	Mode	Range	Standard Deviation	Skew	Kurtosis
STAT3R	Employment status							
FTPTWK	Full-time or Part-time work							
TOTHRS	Total hours worked in a week							
NSECMJ3R	Class							

Install the **Analysis Toolpak** (see Section 3.5.1) and calculate summary statistics for each of the variables in the dataset. Complete Table 4.3 with all the relevant data. Where it is inappropriate to report the mean, median, range, standard deviation, skew or kurtosis, leave the cell in the table blank.

Table 4.3 Descriptive statistics for each variable

Variable Name	Variable Label	Mean	Median	Mode	Range	Standard Deviation	Skew	Kurtosis
SEX	Respondent's gender							
AGEEULR	Age bands in 5-year intervals							
MARSTA3AR	Marital status							
HIQUL15D	Highest qualification							
ETHUK7R	Ethnicity							
ILODEFR	Economic activity							
STAT3R	Employment status							
FTPTWK	Full-time or Part-time work							
TOTHRS	Total hours worked in a week							
NSECMJ3R	Class							

Check Distribution of the Data

Based on the information that you have found, do you think any of the variables in the Quarterly Labour Force Survey (January–March 2015) Teaching Dataset are normally distributed? Explain your answer and create a histogram of the continuous level variable(s) to visually inspect the distribution further.

Further Reading

Bors, D. 2018. Descriptive Statistics. In: Bors. D. *Data Analysis for Social Sciences: Integrating Theory and Practice*. London: Sage, pp. 22–80.

Haaker, M. 2019. *Little Quick Fix: Choose Your Statistical Test*. London: Sage.

MacInnes, J. 2019a. *Little Quick Fix: Know Your Variables.* London: Sage.

Skills Checklist for Chapter 4

Use the checklist provided to track your learning and to highlight areas where you may need to do some additional reading.

	I can do this confidently	I could do this if I had a little more practice	I need more help with this
Differentiate between different levels of data (nominal, ordinal and continuous)			
Identify when it is appropriate to report the mean, median, mode, range and standard deviation			
Identify whether data adopts a normal distribution			
Run Descriptive Statistics in Microsoft Excel			
Use the Countif function in Microsoft Excel			
Create a histogram in Microsoft Excel			

Ideas for Teachers/Instructors

Typical Person in This Room

Get students to collect data on each other and work out what the typical student in the room is like. Students could collect data on favourite colour, number of pets ever owned, number of siblings and age. If you take tape measures to the session, students can also collect data on height or arm length. Ask students to consider the most appropriate descriptive statistics to report for each variable that they collect data for. You may also want to encourage further discussion on data coding and how they intend to deal with missing data. It may also be advantageous to include a variable such as highest level of qualification in the activity and report your own data – this may enable the students to start talking about outliers.

Top Trumps

Get students to create and play with their own Top Trumps as described in Cohen's (2014) paper:

Cohen, R. 2014. Playing with Numbers: Using Top Trumps as an Ice-Breaker and Introduction to Quantitative Methods. *Enhancing Learning in the Social Sciences* 6(2), pp. 21–29.

5

EXPLORING BIVARIATE RELATIONSHIPS: CROSSTABULATIONS AND CHI-SQUARE STATISTIC

Exploring whether respondents belong to different categories and investigating whether they are statistically significantly more likely to belong to one response category compared with another using Microsoft Excel

Colour Code for Chapter:
Amber
Study Skills:
Analysing and interpreting data
Research Methods Skills:
Bivariate analysis, Crosstabulations, Chi-square statistic
Microsoft Excel Skills:
PivotTables, Chi-Square statistic
Datasets Used:
Public Attitudes to Animal Research Survey, 2016

Visit **https://study.sagepub.com/brookfield** to download the datasets used in this chapter.

Chapter Outline

This chapter will introduce bivariate data analysis. Specifically, it will describe when and how to crosstabulate data in Excel. It will also include guidance regarding the assumptions of the chi-square statistic and details of how this can be calculated using Excel.

5.1 Introduction

Often researchers are interested in exploring possible relationships or associations between variables. Specifically, they may wish to investigate how changing one variable impacts on another; this is called 'bivariate data analysis'. In this type of analysis, it is important to differentiate between the 'independent variable' and the 'dependent variable'. The independent variable is the one that the researcher changes or manipulates, while the dependent variable is the one that they observe any subsequent change in. For example, if a researcher were interested in exploring whether there was an association between gender and average pay, gender would be the independent variable and average pay would be the dependent variable. This is because, in this example, the researcher is choosing whether to look at males or females and then seeing what impact this has on average pay.

Researchers formulate hypotheses at the start of their bivariate-level analysis which outline the relationships that they wish to investigate. Usually, you state both a null and an alternative hypothesis. The 'alternative hypothesis' states that there is a statistically significant relationship or association between the independent and dependent variables. Meanwhile, the 'null hypothesis' states that there is not a statistically significant relationship or association between the independent and dependent variables. It is often helpful to draw on the existing academic literature to assist with the development of hypotheses. This literature may also give you an idea or a 'hunch' about the direction or strength of the relationship between the two variables. Using the gender and average pay example introduced earlier, the alternative hypothesis and null hypothesis would be:

Alternative hypothesis: There is a statistically significant difference in the average pay of males and females.

Null hypothesis: There is not a statistically significant difference in the average pay of males and females.

In bivariate level data analysis, we undertake statistical analysis to determine the probability of the null hypothesis being true and subsequently decide whether we can reject it. When testing these hypotheses, we report 'p-values', which indicate the probability of obtaining the observed data if the null hypothesis was true (that there was no statistically significant relationship or association between the independent and dependent variables). Small p-values call to question the null hypothesis, while large p-values support the null hypothesis. If p-values are small we can reject the null hypothesis, but if p-values are large we fail to reject the null hypothesis.

P-values range between 0 and 1. Values less than 0.05 are typically seen as small enough to allow us to reject the null hypothesis and to accept the alternative hypothesis (that there is a statistically significant relationship or association between the independent and dependent variables). Using the threshold of 0.05 means that there is a probability of 0.05 (or 5%) mistakenly rejecting the null hypothesis when it is in fact true (this is why we cannot say that we accept the null hypothesis and must instead use the phrase 'fail to reject the null hypothesis').

While p-values can help inform you whether or not to reject the null hypothesis, they cannot tell you whether any relationship or association observed in the data is meaningful, relevant or important. This is where it is necessary to draw on the existing literature or to consult others to see whether an observed relationship is meaningful in a real-world context. Many amusing examples have been reported where resultant p-values have meant that the null hypothesis has been rejected and the alternative hypothesis has been accepted, though the findings are spurious.

Remember Box 5.1

What is a null hypothesis?

The null hypothesis states that there is no statistically significant difference or association between the variables under investigation. In social research, statistical analysis is undertaken to see whether the null hypothesis can be disproved and rejected (i.e. whether there is in fact a statistically significant difference or association between the variables being studied).

What is an alternative hypothesis?

The alternative hypothesis is a testable statement which outlines that there is a statistically significant difference or association between the variables under investigation.

5.2 One-Tailed versus Two-Tailed Tests

In the statistical tests described in the following chapters, it may be necessary in some instances to specify whether your hypothesis is directional or not (e.g. T-tests). In all the examples shared, the direction of the relationship is not specified and as such, when prompted by Excel, two-tailed tests are selected. Two-tailed tests look at the possibility of difference in both directions, positively and negatively. For example, when comparing the mean value of a dependent variable for two groups, a two-tailed test will look at the possibility that the mean of group 1 is greater than the mean of group 2, as well as the possibility that the mean of group 1 is less than the mean of group 2. When testing for statistical significance using a p-value of 0.05, a two-tailed test assumes that if the mean value of group 2 falls in the bottom 0.25% or top 0.25% of the distribution of group 1, then the means of the two groups are statistically significantly different. Here 0.25% is chosen as half of 0.05 is allocated to each direction (both positive and negative). Meanwhile, one-tailed tests only explore the difference in a specified direction. Two-tailed tests are used much more frequently than one-tailed tests.

5.3 Crosstabulations and Chi-Square Statistic

Crosstabulations (also known as contingency tables) show the distribution of data across categories. Specifically, they allow us to observe and comment upon possible associations between categorical (nominal- or ordinal-level) variables. The chi-square statistic is often calculated after a researcher has produced a crosstabulation. The chi-square statistic is used to see if there is a statistically significant relationship between the categorical variables under exploration. This is done by comparing the observed counts (what the data actually shows) with the expected counts (what the data would show if the variables under investigation were truly independent of one another). Under the null hypothesis, it is stated that there is no difference between the expected and the observed counts, whereas the alternative hypothesis stipulates that there is a statistically significant difference between the expected and observed counts and, therefore, the variables under investigation are not independent of each other. If the latter is the case, it can be concluded that there is a statistically significant association between the variables under investigation.

Excel's 'PivotTables' can be used to create crosstabulations. This chapter includes guidance on how to insert PivotTables into an Excel workbook as well as details on how to interpret the findings. This is followed by information on how to calculate the chi-square statistic in Excel.

5.4 Creating a PivotTable in Excel

In this example, data from the *Public Attitudes to Animal Research Survey, 2016* will be used. Specifically, a crosstabulation will be created to see whether there is an association between a respondent's sex (**sex**) and whether they read tabloid newspapers (**Tabloid**). For the **sex** variable, males are coded as 1 while females are coded as 2. For the **Tabloid** variable a value of 0 indicates that the participant does not read a daily tabloid regularly, whereas a value of 1 indicates that the participant does read a daily tabloid regularly.

It can be advantageous to copy and paste the key variables of interest into a new worksheet. Once your variables are in the new worksheet, highlight them and under the '**Insert**' tab, select '**PivotTable**' (see Figure 5.1). This process will open a new window.

Figure 5.1 Inserting a PivotTable in Excel

In this new window, ensure that your data is highlighted and then select the output area where you would like your PivotTable to appear. You can select for your PivotTable to appear on the same worksheet or in a new worksheet within your workbook (see Figure 5.2). In this example, the PivotTable will be inserted into the same worksheet.

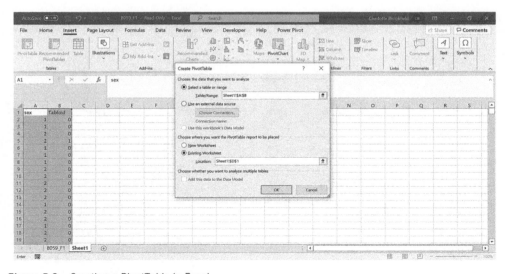

Figure 5.2 Creating a PivotTable in Excel

This will open a new dialog window on the right-hand side of the screen, as shown in Figure 5.3. Under the heading '**Rows**', drag and drop the independent variable. In this case, the independent variable is **sex**. In the '**Columns**' box drag and drop the dependent variable. In this example, the dependent variable is **Tabloid**. Then, drag and drop the independent variable (**sex**) under the '**Values**' box.

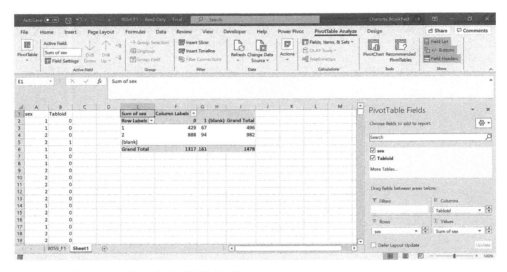

Figure 5.3   Completing '**PivotTable Fields**' in Excel

You will notice that under the 'Values' box in the 'PivotTable Fields' window, the variable states '**Sum of sex**'. This needs to be changed to '**Count**'. The count will

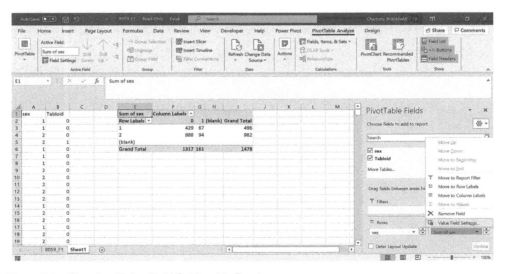

Figure 5.4   Changing '**Value Field Settings**' in Excel

tell you the frequency with which each sex reported reading or not reading daily tabloid papers on a regularly basis. To change the sum to count, click the drop-down arrow next to the variable name and select '**Value Field Settings**' (see Figure 5.4).

This will open a new window (Figure 5.5). Under the '**Summarize Values By**' tab, select '**Count**' from the menu. Then click **OK**.

Summarize Values By > Count > OK

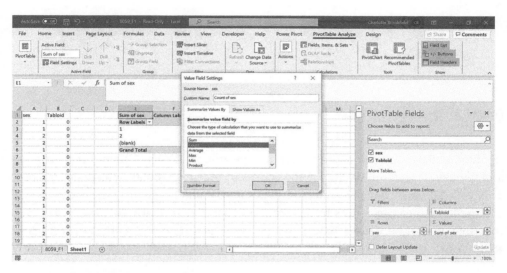

Figure 5.5 Summarising values by **Count** in Excel

The resultant crosstabulation is depicted in Figure 5.6. The columns in the crosstabulation represent whether or not the respondents regularly read a daily tabloid paper, whereas the rows in the crosstabulation represent whether respondents reported being male or female. The grand totals at the bottom of the table depict the number of respondents in the whole sample who did and did not report regularly reading a daily tabloid paper. Meanwhile, the grand totals on the right of the table depict the total number of males and females in the survey sample. In a crosstabulation, it should always be the case that your dependent variable is organised in columns and your independent variable is organised in rows.

Figure 5.6 shows that out of the 496 males (coded as 1) in the survey sample, 429 reported not regularly reading a daily tabloid paper (coded as 0). Meanwhile, the remaining 67 males reported that they did regularly read a daily tabloid paper (coded as 1). Similarly, out of the 491 female participants (coded as 2), 444 reported not regularly reading a daily tabloid paper (coded as 0), while only 47 females reported that they did regularly read daily tabloid papers (coded as 1).

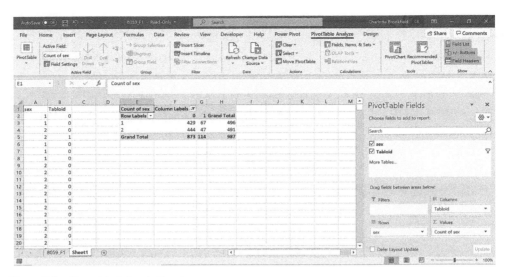

Figure 5.6   Crosstabulation in Excel

In order to make easy comparisons between the groups, in this instance between males and females, it is useful to change the counts in the crosstabulation into percentages. This will tell you what percentage of males and females regularly read daily tabloid papers. To change the counts to percentages, click '**Value Field Settings**' again and this time, under the '**Show Values As**' tab, use the drop-down menu to select '**% of Row Total**' (see Figure 5.7).

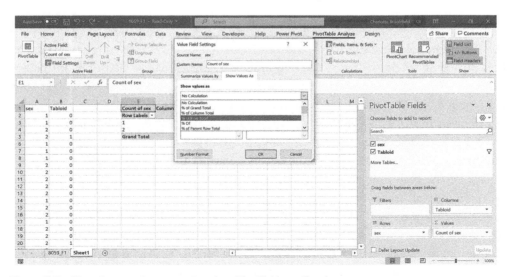

Figure 5.7   Changing count to percentage in a PivotTable on Excel

Click **OK** and your table will update (see Figure 5.8). The new crosstabulation shows that 86.5% of males reported not regularly reading daily tabloids; this is in comparison with 90.4% of female respondents who reported not regularly reading daily tabloid newspapers.

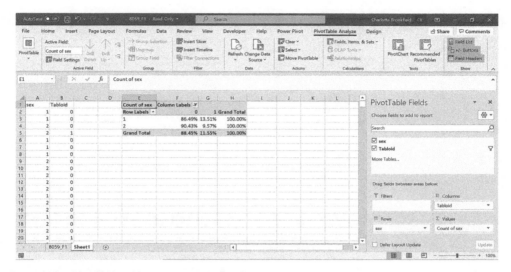

Figure 5.8 PivotTable with percentages in Excel

5.5 Chi-Square Statistic in Excel

As the chi-square test compares the expected and observed cell counts, in order to calculate the chi-square statistic, it is necessary to create another PivotTable with the expected cell counts. The expected cell counts tell us the frequency we would expect to see for each group (in this instance, the number of males and females regularly reading daily tabloid newspapers), if the null hypothesis were true and there was no statistically significant difference between the groups (males and females).

To calculate the expected cell counts, copy the crosstabulation with the count data (not the percentages). Then, paste the table using the paste values option as shown in Figure 5.9.

Next, delete the data from the centre of the table, keeping only the total values. To calculate the expected cell count for a given cell, multiply the column total by the row total and divide it by the grand total (see Figure 5.10). In this example, to calculate the expected cell count for males who do not regularly read daily tabloid papers, the cell (F12) containing the column total (873) is multiplied by the cell (H10) containing the row total (496) and then divided by the grand total (987) in cell (H12). This process is repeated for each of the central cells in the table.

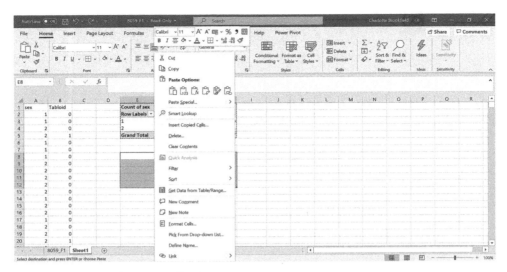

Figure 5.9 Paste values option in Excel

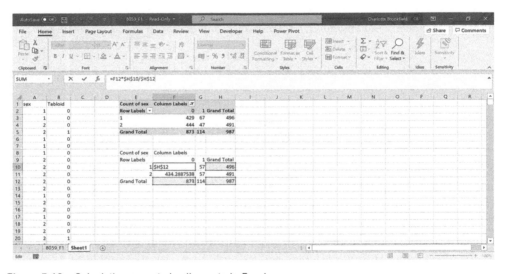

Figure 5.10 Calculating expected cell counts in Excel

An assumption of the chi-square tests is that all the cells have expected cell counts greater than 5. If this assumption is violated, it may be necessary to recode variables to combine response categories. In this example, the assumption is met and there is no need to recode either of the variables.

In Excel, you need to calculate the p-value for your chi-square statistic prior to calculating the chi-square statistic itself. To calculate the p-value for the chi-square statistic, use the formula '=CHISQ.TEST(Observed counts: Expected counts)'. This is shown in Figure 5.11.

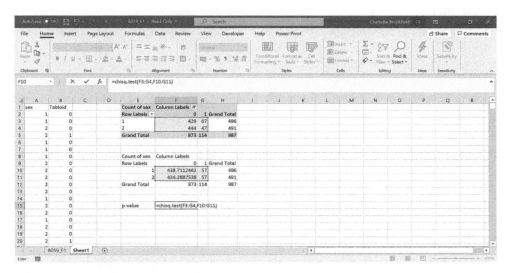

Figure 5.11 The p-value for the chi-square statistic in Excel

In the example shown in this figure, the resultant p-value is 0.053 and therefore slightly larger than the set alpha value of 0.05. As a result, we can conclude that there is not a statistically significant difference between the number of males and females that regularly read daily tabloid news. This means that we fail to reject the null hypothesis.

Before you can calculate the chi-square statistic you also need to calculate the degrees of freedom. Degrees of freedom denote how many cells in your crosstabulation can vary at any given time. Degrees of freedom are calculated by subtracting 1 from the number of columns in your table, multiplied by the number of rows in your table minus 1, thus:

Degrees of freedom: (Number of columns − 1) * (Number of rows − 1)

In the example used in this chapter, the crosstabulation contains two columns with data and two rows with data. Therefore, the degrees of freedom would be 1.

Degrees of freedom: (Number of columns − 1) * (Number of rows − 1)

= (2 − 1) * (2 − 1)

= 1 * 1

= 1

To calculate the chi-square statistic, you need to use the 'CHISQ.INV.RT' formula in Excel, followed by the p-value and the degrees of freedom. For the present example, you would insert the following:

=CHISQ.INV.RT(0.053, 1)

=3.74392

Rather than typing the numbers into the formula, you can, alternatively, click the cells which contain the p-value and the degrees of freedom in your Excel worksheet (see Figure 5.12).

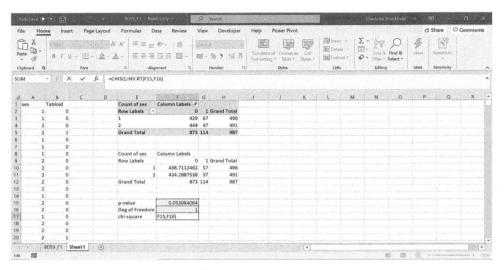

Figure 5.12 Chi-square test statistic in Excel

The results of the chi-square test in this example would be presented as follows: $(x^2=3.74, 1d.f, p>0.05)$, where x^2 denotes the chi-square statistic, d.f refers to the number of degrees of freedom and $p>0.05$ tells the reader that the result was not statistically significant.

Create a Crosstabulation and Calculate a Chi-Square Statistic

1. Download the *Public Attitudes to Animal Research Survey, 2016* dataset

To access the *Public Attitudes to Animal Research Survey, 2016* data, you need to visit the UK Data Service website using the address below:

www.ukdataservice.ac.uk

Once the webpage has loaded, select '**Get Data**' and, in the search box, type the following:

Public Attitudes to Animal Research, 2016

Select the 2016 dataset. In the new window, select the purple box labelled '**Access Data**'. Select the option to download the TAB file format of the data. Save the TAB data file on your computer. Then, open Excel and select '**File**' and '**Open**'. Browse for the TAB file, making sure that '**All Files**' are visible (the default is 'All Excel Files'). Once you have located the correct file, select '**Open**'. After this a series of windows will appear. Select '**Next**' to each of these and then choose '**Finish**'.

2. Create a crosstabulation and calculate a chi-square statistic using Excel

Repeat the analysis shown in this chapter but, this time, explore whether there is a statistically significant difference between the percentage of male and female participants (**sex**) who reported regularly reading a daily broadsheet paper (**broadsheet**).

In this activity, males are coded as 1 and females are coded as 2. Those who reported regularly reading a daily broadsheet paper are coded as 1, while those who reported not regularly reading a daily broadsheet paper are coded as 0.

Write your null and alternative hypotheses below:

Null hypothesis:

....

....

Alternative hypothesis:

....

....

Copy your PivotTable in Excel to complete the crosstabulation in Table 5.1.

Table 5.1   Crosstabulation of sex and whether a respondent regularly reads a daily broadsheet newspaper

	Read Broadsheet	Don't Read Broadsheet	Total
Male			
Female			
Total			

What percentage of females reported regularly reading a daily broadsheet paper?

....

What percentage of males reported regularly reading a daily broadsheet paper?

....

(Continued)

Calculate the chi-square statistic for these variables. Is there a statistically significant relationship between sex and whether a participant regularly reads a daily broadsheet paper?

....

Further Reading

MacInnes, J. 2019b. *Little Quick Fix: Statistical Significance*. London: Sage.

Skills Checklist for Chapter 5

Use the checklist provided to track your learning and to highlight areas where you may need to do some additional reading.

	I can do this confidently	I could do this if I had a little more practice	I need more help with this
Create a PivotTable			
Interpret a crosstabulation			
Calculate a chi-square statistic in Microsoft Excel			
Interpret a chi-square statistic			

Ideas for Teachers/Instructors

Human Crosstabulations

One way to demonstrate to students how crosstabulations work is to allow them to create human crosstabulations in the classroom. To facilitate this, choose two questions from a pre-existing survey. It is usually simplest to choose questions that have only two response categories each, otherwise your human crosstabulation can get very large! Read out the questions and ask the students to write down their answers. Based on their answers, students should then go to different corners/areas of the room. Explain to the students that Excel organises the data in this way when it produces a crosstabulation. As an extension, you could collate the data for the questions from the students and input it into Excel to confirm that the human crosstabulation matches the Excel version.

This exercise can also be completed in small groups on tables using picture cards with celebrities, cartoon characters, and so on. For instance, you can ask students to place all cards with pictures of male celebrities wearing glasses in the top left corner of the table, pictures of males not wearing glasses in the top right corner, pictures of females wearing glasses in the bottom left corner and pictures of females not wearing glasses in the bottom right corner. Ask the students to count how many picture cards they have in each of the piles and to present the information in a crosstabulation. Again, they could verify their answers using Excel.

Explaining Degrees of Freedom

Explain degrees of freedom using the hat example from Minitab (2016). In this example, students are encouraged to imagine that they have seven different hats and that on each day of the week, they want to wear a different hat (to avoid outfit repetition!). This means on Monday (day 1) they have a choice of seven hats to wear. By Tuesday (day 2), they have six hats to choose from. Wednesday (day 3) they have five hats to choose from, Thursday (day 4) they have four hats to choose from, Friday (day 5) they have three hats to choose from and Saturday (day 6) they have two hats to choose from. By Sunday (day 7), they have no choice – there is only one more hat that they can wear to avoid outfit repetition. This means that on six out of the seven days they had a choice, but on the final day, they did not.

This can be used as an introduction to degrees of freedom. Like the student who wanted to wear a different hat each day, in a crosstabulation there are only so many cells where there is a choice or the ability to vary. Once a proportion of the cells in the crosstabulation table are full, the values for the other cells are determined and there is no choice left. For instance, in the example in Table 5.2, once we know that the number of males wearing glasses is 7, we can work out the number of males who do not wear glasses and the number of females who do and do not wear glasses. Therefore, in this example, only one cell in the table could vary or change until we were left with no choice.

Table 5.2 Explaining degrees of freedom

	Glasses	No Glasses	Total
Males	7		10
Females			10
	10	10	20

This can be confirmed using the formula to calculate degrees of freedom: $=$(Number of columns $-$ 1)*(Number of rows $-$ 1). In this example, 1*1 would indicate we have 1 degree of freedom.

Minitab. 2016. *What Are Degrees of Freedom in Statistics?* Available at: https://blog.minitab.com/blog/statistics-and-quality-data-analysis/what-are-degrees-of-freedom-in-statistics [Accessed 30 July 2019].

6

T-TESTS, ANOVA TEST AND NON-PARAMETRIC EQUIVALENTS

Exploring whether two independent groups are statistically significantly different using Microsoft Excel

Colour Code for Chapter:
Amber
Study Skills:
Analysing and interpreting data
Research Methods Skills:
Bivariate analysis, T-tests, Mann–Whitney U tests, ANOVA test, Kruskal–Wallis test, F-tests
Microsoft Excel Skills:
F-Test, T-Test, Anova test, Rank.Avg, Sum, Min, Power
Datasets Used:
Living Costs and Food Survey, 2013: Unrestricted Access Teaching Dataset
Quarterly Labour Force Survey Household Dataset, January–March, 2015

Visit **https://study.sagepub.com/brookfield** to download the datasets used in this chapter.

─Chapter Outline─

This chapter will describe different statistical tests that you can undertake in order to explore whether there are statistically significant differences between different groups in your dataset. It will explain the assumptions of the different tests and the key information that you need to deduce to decide which test is most appropriate. The chapter will also include instructions on how to undertake these statistical tests in Excel and how to analyse and interpret the resultant data.

6.1 Introduction

A T-test compares the mean scores of a dependent continuous level variable for two groups. For example, you could use a T-test to compare the mean test scores of male and female students. For a T-test, your null hypothesis states that there is no statistically significant difference in the mean values of the two groups, while the alternative hypothesis states that there is a statistically significant difference in the mean values of the two groups. Using the example of comparing test scores, the null and alternative hypotheses in this scenario would be:

Null hypothesis: There is no statistically significant difference in the mean test scores of male and female students.

Alternative hypothesis: There is a statistically significant difference in the mean test scores of male and female students.

For a T-test the dependent variable must be continuous, and the independent variable must be a dichotomous categorical variable (a categorical variable with two possible response categories). One of the assumptions of the T-test is that the dependent variable is normally distributed for both of the groups under investigation (see Section 4.5). To explore the distribution of the data for both groups, it may be necessary to create a histogram of the data and to look at the skew and kurtosis.

Similarly, an ANOVA test compares the mean scores of a dependent continuous variable; however, the ANOVA test is used in situations where you are exploring three or more groups at the same time. For instance, you may wish to compare the mean test scores of three different classes within one school. Again, for an ANOVA test, the null hypothesis would stipulate that there is not a statistically significant difference in the mean values of the different groups, while the alternative hypothesis would state that there is a statistically significant difference in the mean values of the different groups. For instance:

Null hypothesis: There is no statistically significant difference in the mean scores between the classes.

Alternative hypothesis: There is a statistically significant difference in the mean scores between the classes.

For an ANOVA (analysis of variance) test, the dependent variable must be continuous, and the independent variable should be a categorical variable with three or more response categories. As with the T-test, an assumption of the ANOVA test is that the dependent variable is normally distributed for each of the groups under exploration. It is important to note that an ANOVA test does not tell you between which of the groups there is a statistically significant difference. Rather, the test simply informs you whether or not there are statistically significant differences in the mean values of the groups. If you were interested in finding out which groups have statistically significant differences, you would need to use a post-hoc test after undertaking the ANOVA test.

In situations where the assumption of normality is violated and therefore it is not possible to use either a T-test or ANOVA test, there are equivalent tests that can be used which do not rely on this assumption. These tests are called the Mann–Whitney U Test and the Kruskal–Wallis test.

The Mann–Whitney U Test compares the distribution of data across two groups and is considered an alternative to the T-test when you have non-normally distributed data or in situations where you have an ordinal-level dependent variable. The null hypothesis for a Mann–Whitney U Test is that there is no statistically significant difference in the population distributions between the two groups being explored, and the alternative hypothesis for a Mann–Whitney U Test is that there is a statistically significant difference in the population distributions between the two groups under investigation. The resultant U statistic ranges from 0 to n_1 multiplied by n_2, where n_1 is the number of observations in group 1 and n_2 the number of observations in group 2. The closer to 0 the final statistic is, the more likely it is that the distributions between the two groups are different and the greater the support you have for your alternative hypothesis.

A Kruskal–Wallis test compares the distribution of the dependent variable across three or more groups. For this test, the dependent variable is either continuous and not normally distributed or ordinal. The independent variable is categorical and should contain three or more response categories. The null hypothesis in a Kruskal–Wallis test states that the population distributions are not statistically significantly different, and the alternative hypothesis states that the population distributions are statistically significantly different. Like the ANOVA test, the Kruskal–Wallis test cannot tell you between which groups there are differences.

Importantly, as the Mann–Whitney U Test and Kruskal–Wallis test do not rely on the assumption of normality, they are considered less accurate and do not have the same statistical power as the T-test and ANOVA test. Therefore, in situations where the data is not normally distributed but the sample size is larger than 15 for each of the groups under investigation, it is possible to use the T-test or ANOVA test.

In the examples shown in this chapter, the assumption of normality is ignored, and the same data is used for the T-test, Mann–Whitney U, ANOVA and Kruskal–Wallis test examples. This is to allow the reader to understand the differences in steps needed to undertake the tests and the difference in the presentation of the data for each of the tests.

Prior to undertaking these tests, it is necessary to filter the dependent variable by the grouping independent variable (see Section 3.13) and explore it in detail. This allows you to see whether a continuous-level variable is normally distributed for each group under investigation. You will also need the continuous dependent variable filtered by the grouping variable in order to determine whether the spread of the data is similar between the groups. This is known as an F-test and is described below.

6.2 F-tests

Before conducting a T-test, you need to deduce whether the spread of the continuous level variable is similar for each of the groups under exploration. The F-test tells you whether the spread, or variance, of the data in the groups is similar or not. For an F-test the null hypothesis states that there is no statistically significant difference in the variance between the two groups under investigation, while the alternative hypothesis states that there is a statistically significant difference in the variance between the two groups which you are exploring. If the resultant F-value is greater than the F critical value, then the null hypothesis is rejected and we assume that the variance is unequal. When the F-value is less than the F critical value, we fail to reject the null hypothesis and assume that the variance is equal between the two groups.

In this example, the Quarterly Labour Force Survey (January–March 2015: Unrestricted Access Teaching Dataset) is used. Here, we will investigate whether there is a statistically significant difference in the mean number of hours worked in a week between males and females using an F-test. The grouping independent variable in this example is sex (**SEX**) and the continuous dependent variable is total hours worked in the reference week (**TOTHRS**). For the grouping independent variable, a '1' refers to a male respondent, while a '2' denotes a female respondent. As in Chapter 3, the continuous level variable **TOTHRS** has been restricted to values between 0 and 60. In this example, the null hypothesis and alternative hypothesis are as follows:

Null hypothesis: The variance in the number of hours worked is not statistically significantly different between male and female participants.

Alternative hypothesis: The variance in the number of hours worked is statistically significantly different between male and female participants.

To undertake the F-test, click the '**Data**' tab and select '**Data Analysis**'. This will open a new window with a list of different tests. From this list, select '**F-Test Two-Sample for Variances**' and click **OK**.

Data > Data Analysis > F-Test Two-Sample for Variances > OK

You then need to enter the data that you wish to analyse. For each group, you will need to highlight the continuous level data and insert the range into the 'Variable Range' box. In Figure 6.1, the Variable 1 Range is the total hours worked for the females in the survey sample and the Variable 2 Range is the total hours worked for the males in the survey sample. In this instance, the '**Labels**' box has been ticked as the column titles have been included in the variable range. You also need to choose where you want the output to appear. In the example in Figure 6.1, the option has been selected to appear in column E on the same worksheet as the data. Once all the options are completed, select **OK**.

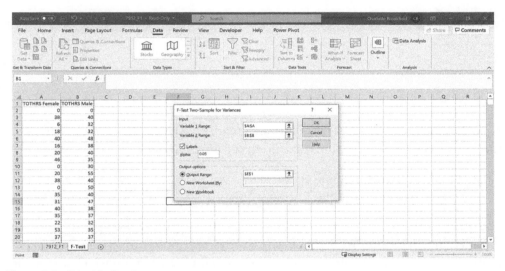

Figure 6.1 F-test in Excel

The resultant output contains key information that is needed to undertake the analysis. Figure 6.2 shows the mean number of hours worked in each group. On average males worked 34.9 hours a week compared to females who worked 26.4 hours. The variance for each group is also displayed in this table. If the variance is similar for both groups, we would expect the F-value to be smaller than the F critical value. If the variance between the groups is dissimilar, we would expect the F-value to be greater than the F critical value. In this example, the output also shows that the F-value is 0.95 and that the F critical value is 0.96. As the F-value is smaller than the F critical value, the null hypothesis cannot be rejected and it must be assumed that the variance in the number of hours worked each week is the same for the males and females in the sample. This means that when we undertake the T-test we must select the 't-test: Two-Sample Assuming Equal Variances' option as opposed to the 't-test: Two-Sample Assuming Unequal Variances' one. If the F-value is larger than the F critical value, then you select the 't-test: Two-Sample Assuming Unequal Variances' option.

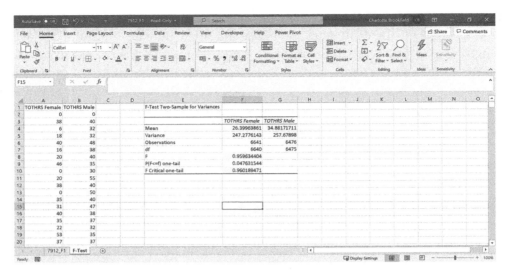

Figure 6.2 F-test interpretation in Excel

Note that the F statistic is calculated by dividing the variance of one of the groups by the variance of the other group as shown in the formula below:

$$\text{F statistic} = \frac{\text{Variance of group 1}}{\text{Variance of group 2}}$$

The group with the least variance should form the numerator (top number) in this formula and the group with the greatest variance should form the denominator (bottom number). Excel automatically assumes that the first group which appears in your worksheet (the one on the left) has the least variance and that the second group (the one on the right) has the greatest variance. Subsequently, Excel uses the variance for the group on the left as the numerator and the variance for the group on the right as the denominator when calculating the F statistic. However, if this is incorrect, it will be necessary for you to repeat the test and swap the input ranges over so that the variable with the greatest variance appears in the Variable 2 input range and the variable with the least variance appears in the Variable 1 input range.

The F statistic should never be greater than 1; if Excel returns an F statistic greater than 1 it suggests that it has used the groups the wrong way round in the formula and that you need to swap over the variable input ranges. The closer to 1 the value of the F statistic, the more similar the variance. If the F statistic is equal to 1, you can conclude that the variance between the two groups is equal.

6.3 T-tests in Excel

The '**Data Analysis**' menu in Excel allows you to undertake a T-test quickly and easily. Make sure that you have the '**Data Analysis Toolpak**' plug-in installed (see Section 3.5.1).

To run a T-test, under the '**Data**' tab, select '**Data Analysis**'. This will open a new window with a list of statistical tests. Depending on the results of the F-test, you need to select either '**t-Test: Two-Sample Assuming Unequal Variances**' or '**t-Test: Two-Sample Assuming Equal Variances**'. In this example, equal variance is assumed and therefore, in Figure 6.3, we have scrolled down and selected '**t-Test: Two-Sample Assuming Equal Variances**'. Click **OK** (see Figure 6.3).

Data > Data Analysis > t-Test: Two-Sample Assuming Equal Variances > OK

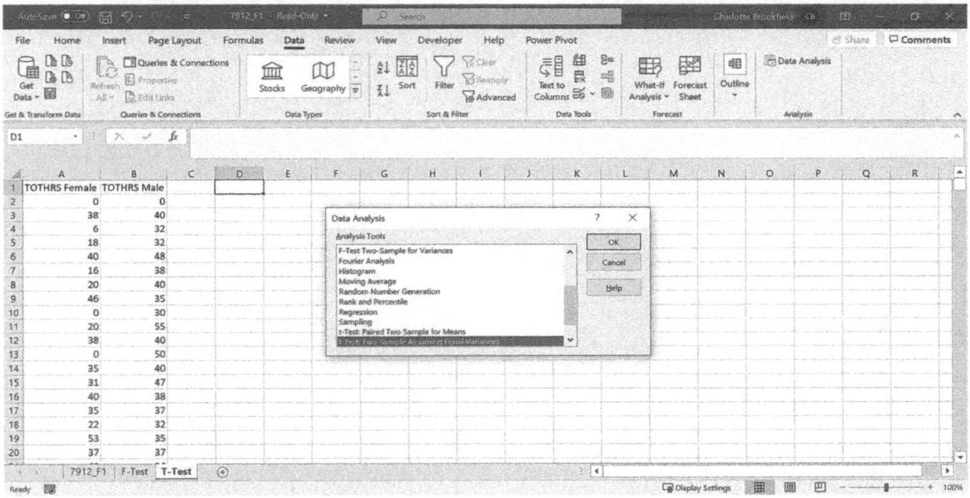

Figure 6.3 Selecting 't-Test: Two-Sample Assuming Equal Variances' in Excel

In the new window, begin by selecting the first input range. For this example, Variable 1 Range is the values for the female participants. Following this, select the values for the Variable 2 Range, which will be the values of your dependent variable for the second group of respondents under exploration. In this example, this would be the total number of hours worked by the male participants. If you have included the column headings in your selections, it is important to select the '**Labels**' box. Finally, you will need to decide where you would like the output from the test to appear. In the example in Figure 6.4, it has been decided that the output will appear on the same page. Click **OK** to run the test.

The T-test statistic is referred to as the 't Stat' in the new output (see Figure 6.5). In the present example, the T-test statistic, or the 't Stat' is –30.8. The closer to 0 the T-Test statistic is, the more likely it is that there is not a statistically significant difference between the means of both groups.

In order to deduce whether the T-test statistic is statistically significant, it is necessary to look at the p-value in the output table; this has been highlighted in Figure 6.5. Note that, as the direction of the relationship is not specified in the hypothesis, the two-tail p-value is reported (see Section 5.2). If the p-value is smaller than 0.05 then you can conclude that there is a statistically significant difference in the means between the two groups. As explained in Chapter 5, the threshold of 0.05 is often used in the social sciences to determine whether a relationship is statistically significant or not. In this example, the p-value is smaller than 0.05 and therefore we must reject the null hypothesis that there is no statistically significant difference in the mean number of hours worked between males and females in the sample.

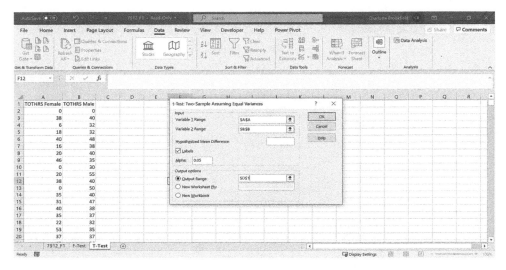

Figure 6.4 T-test in Excel

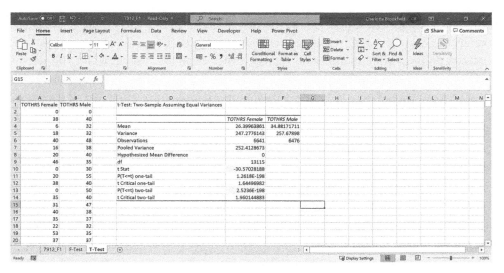

Figure 6.5 T-test output in Excel

Alternatively, the p-value for a T-test can be calculated using the '=T.TEST' formula. This formula needs to be followed by the coordinates of the column with the first group's data and then the coordinates of the column with the second group's data. This is followed by the number 2 to indicate that you are comparing the means of two separate groups and then either a 1 or 2 to indicate whether the variance is unequal or equal respectively. This is shown in Figure 6.6.

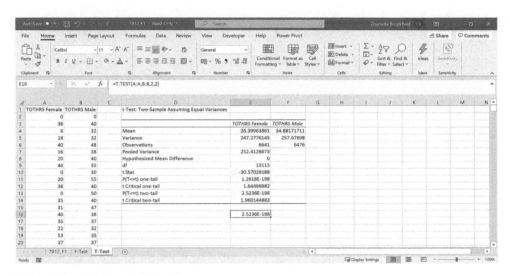

Figure 6.6 T-test formula in Excel

The process for undertaking a T-test and analysing the data where the variance is unequal is the same; however, you must select '**t-Test: Two-Sample Assuming Unequal Variances**' from the '**Data Analysis**' menu.

Remember Box 6.1

Standard Form or Scientific Notation

Standard form or scientific notion is used to express very large or very small numbers using powers of 10. It often looks much neater than writing very large or very small numbers in full and can therefore be useful. Standard form is written as M * 10E, where 'M' is a number between 1 and 10 and 'E' is a positive or negative number which denotes the power. Written in standard form, the number 365.98 would appear as $3.6598 * 10^2$. This means that when 10 is squared (or multiplied by itself) and then multiplied by 3.6598, you will reach the original long number 365.98. Written in standard form the number 0.036 598 would appear as $3.6598 * 10^{-2}$. This means that

(Continued)

when 10 is squared (or multiplied by itself) and then 3.6598 is divided by the resultant answer (100), you reach the long, original, small number of 0.036 598. The larger or smaller the number, the more helpful standard form is at saving space. If the value of 'E' is positive it means that standard form calculation will give you a large number, whereas if the value of 'E' is negative, the standard form calculation will give you a small number. This is because, when the value of 'E' is positive, you are multiplying by a power of 10 (therefore increasing the value of the number), while, when the value of 'E' is negative, you are dividing by a power of 10 (therefore decreasing the value of the number).

Excel uses standard form to help save space in worksheets. In Figure 6.5, the p-value for T-test is expressed in standard form as 2.5236E-198. This means that if you multiplied 10 by itself 198 times and then divided 2.5236 by your answer you would know the actual, very small p-value. In this example, dividing 2.5236 by 100 (10^2) would already mean that our p-value would be below 0.05, therefore we can confidently conclude that the difference in means between the two groups is statistically significant.

6.4 Mann–Whitney U Tests in Excel

If the continuous level variable that you are exploring is not normally distributed for the two groups under investigation, or if your dependent variable is an ordinal level variable, it is necessary to undertake a Mann–Whitney U Test. This test compares the distribution of the data between the two groups. Unfortunately, the Analysis ToolPak does not include the Mann–Whitney U Test. This means that you need to undertake a number of steps to complete the analysis.

The overall formula for the Mann–Whitney U statistic is:

$$U = R - \frac{n(n+1)}{2}$$

where R is equal to the sum of the ranks and n is equal to the number of observations. You need to calculate the Mann–Whitney U statistic for both of your groups – in this example the statistic is calculated for both males and females. The calculation that gives you the lowest value is the one that you report.

To aid the analysis, it is important to produce descriptive statistics for the variable under investigation for each group. In this example, the data has been rearranged so that you can see the total hours worked by males and females in the reference week in separate columns. In addition, as shown in Figure 6.7, summary statistics for both males and females have been calculated (see Section 4.6). These summary statistics provide us with important information that we need to undertake the Mann–Whitney U Test, including the number of observations.

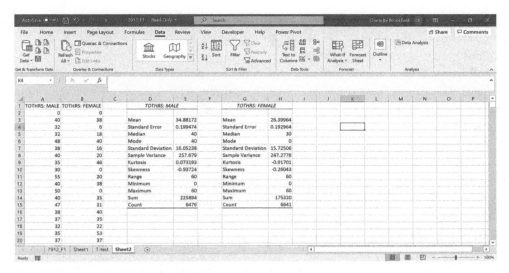

Figure 6.7 Descriptive statistics for groups under exploration using Excel

As we are assuming that the data is not normally distributed, it is necessary to rank the continuous level data for each group from lowest to highest before we proceed with the analysis. This is because the Mann–Whitney U Test compares the ranked means of the groups. To rank the data, you need to use the rank formula on the unsorted data. This is achieved by using the '=RANK.AVG' formula, followed by the reference of the first cell in your data and the table range, followed by the number 1. For instance, in the example in Figure 6.8, the formula appears as '=RANK.AVG(B2, B:B, 1)'. This tells Excel to assign a rank to the value appearing in cell B2, based on the values presented

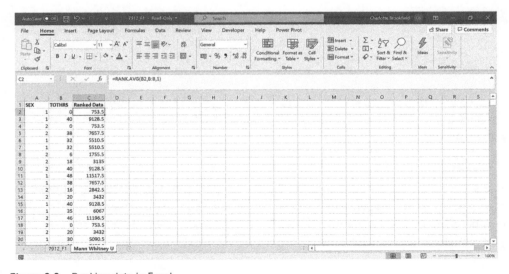

Figure 6.8 Ranking data in Excel

in column B. The '1' at the end of the formula tells Excel that the ranks should be assigned in ascending order, with the lowest values given the lowest ranks and the highest values given the highest ranks.

Following this, you need to sum the ranks for each group – the males and the females. This can be done using the '=SUMIF' formula. This formula tells Excel to summate the values for a particular group. The formula should be followed by the range of the grouping variable. In this example, the grouping variable (**SEX**) appears in column A. Following this, you need to tell Excel the criteria for counting. First, we want Excel to calculate the sum of the ranks for the males only. Males are coded as 1 in the dataset; therefore it is necessary to insert a '1' into the formula. After this, you need to tell Excel the location of the values that need summating. In the example in Figure 6.9, the ranked data for total hours worked in the reference week is in column C. Therefore, the final formula for calculating the sum of the ranks for the male participants appears as '=SUMIF (A:A, 1, C:C)'. To calculate the sum of ranks for the female participants, the '1' in the formula must be substituted for a '2'. This is because females are coded as '2' in the dataset. In this example, the sum of the ranks for the male group is 49 779 581 and the sum of the ranks for the female group is 36 254 822 (see Figure 6.9).

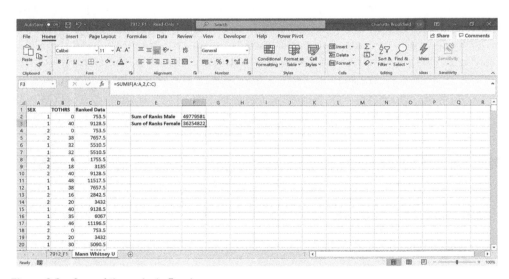

Figure 6.9 Sum of the ranks in Excel

The second piece of information needed to complete the formula is the number of observations of the dependent variable for each group. In this example, this is the number of males and the number of females that you have data on for the total number of hours worked. Remember that you calculate the U statistic for each group under exploration, therefore it is necessary at this stage to report the count for both groups. The count for each group can be seen in the summary statistics produced in Figure 6.7. In this example, we have data on the total hours worked in the reference week for 6476 males and 6641 females.

The final piece of information needed to complete the formula is the count for each group plus one. In the example shown here, this would mean adding 1 to 6476 for the male group and adding 1 to 6641 for the female group. Again, it is necessary to repeat the process for both of the groups under exploration.

Once you have all this information, you can substitute the numbers into the equation. For instance, in the example below the U statistic for males is calculated:

$$U = R - \frac{n(n+1)}{2}$$
$$= 49\,779\,581 - \frac{6476(6476+1)}{2}$$
$$= 49\,779\,581 - \frac{6476(6477)}{2}$$
$$= 49\,779\,581 - \frac{41\,945\,052}{2}$$
$$= 49\,779\,581 - 20\,972\,526$$
$$= 28\,807\,055$$

This process needs to be repeated for the second group. In this example, the U statistic for females would be calculated as shown below:

$$U = R - \frac{n(n+1)}{2}$$
$$= 36\,254\,822 - \frac{6641(6641+1)}{2}$$
$$= 36\,254\,822 - \frac{6641(6642)}{2}$$
$$= 36\,254\,822 - \frac{41\,109\,522}{2}$$
$$= 36\,254\,822 - 22\,054\,761$$
$$= 14\,200\,061$$

These calculations can be performed in Excel (see Figure 6.10) or with a calculator.

You then need to identify the smallest number out of the two resultant statistics. You can use the '=MIN' formula to help you if you prefer (see example in Figure 6.11).

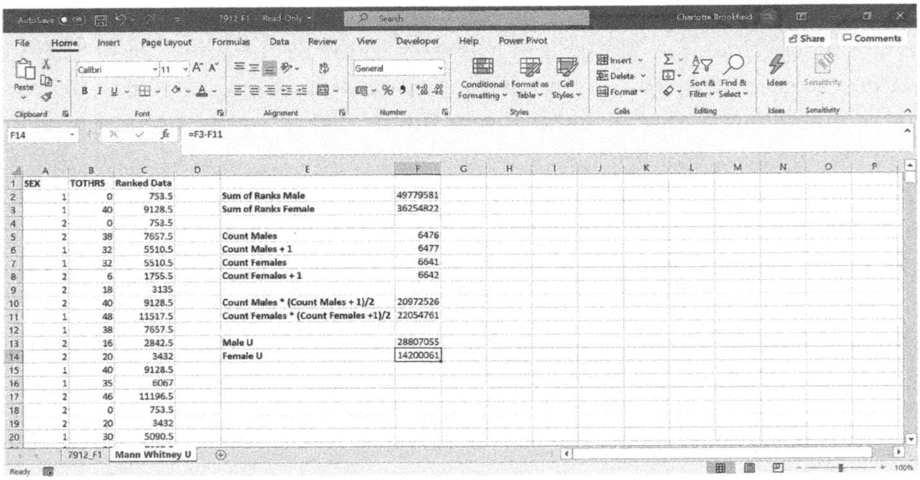

Figure 6.10 Calculating Mann–Whitney U statistic in Excel

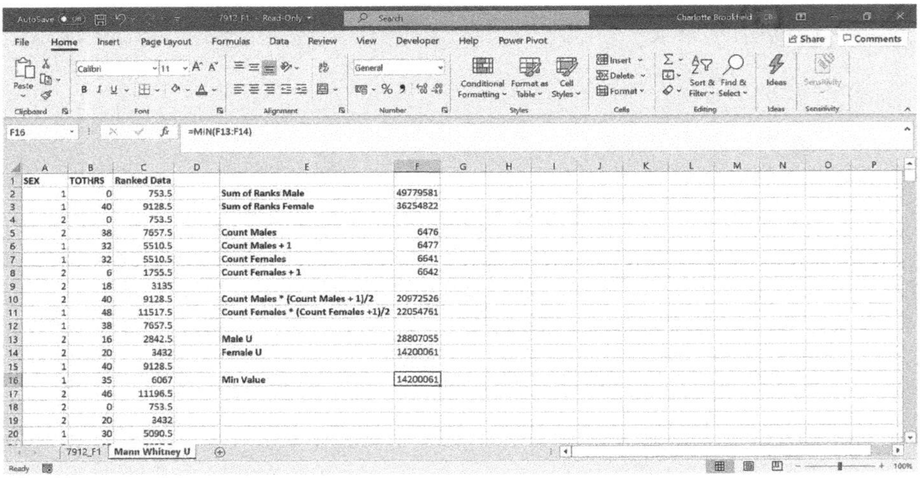

Figure 6.11 Finding minimum value in Excel

The remaining steps are used to determine whether the U statistic is statistically significant. This is done using a Mann–Whitney U significance table which can be found online. To read the significance table, you need to look up where the sample sizes for the two groups meet. If the U statistic is less than this value, then you are able to reject the null hypothesis.

6.5 ANOVA Test in Excel

When you have multiple groups (more than two) that you wish to compare and the continuous level data is normally distributed for each group, then you can undertake an ANOVA test to compare the mean for each group.

In this example, the total number of hours worked in the reference week is compared according to the marital status of the respondents of the Quarterly Labour Force Survey, January–March, 2015: Unrestricted Access Teaching Dataset. The independent variable in this example is **Marsta3r** (marital status) and the group options are **'Single/Never married'** (1), **'Married/Cohabiting/Civil Partner'** (2), or **'Divorced/Widowed/Previously in Civil Partnership'** (3). The dependent variable is **TOTHRS** (total hours worked in the reference week).

Before undertaking an ANOVA test in Excel, it is necessary to rearrange the data. In Figure 6.12, the data for the total number of hours worked in the reference week has been sorted by group.

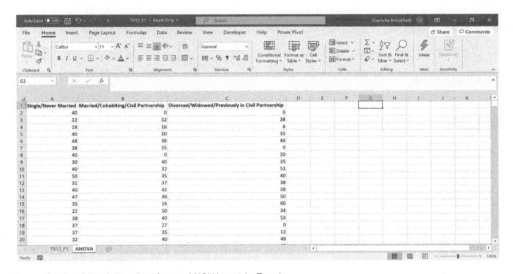

Figure 6.12 Organising data for an ANOVA test in Excel

Once the data is rearranged, you are able to carry out an ANOVA test. To undertake the test, select the **'Data'** tab from the top toolbar. Click **'Data Analysis Toolpak'**. This will open a new window. In this new window, scroll down and select **'Anova: Single Factor'**, and click **OK**. These steps are shown in Figure 6.13.

Data > Data Analysis > Anova: Single Factor > OK

Once you have selected the 'Anova: Single Factor' test, a new menu will open (see Figure 6.14). To begin, you need to enter the **'Input Range'** – this is the data that you have rearranged. If you have included the column headings in the **'Input Range'**, make sure that you select the **'Labels'** box. Then, select where you would like the output of the ANOVA test to appear. In the example in Figure 6.14, the output appears on the same worksheet. Once all this information is completed, select **OK**. The output will then appear.

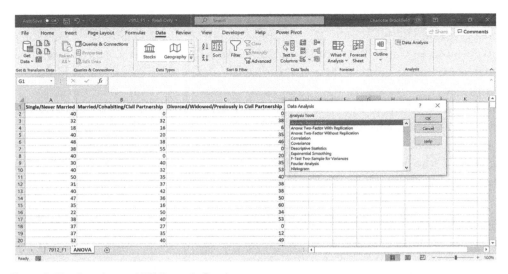

Figure 6.13 Running an ANOVA test in Excel

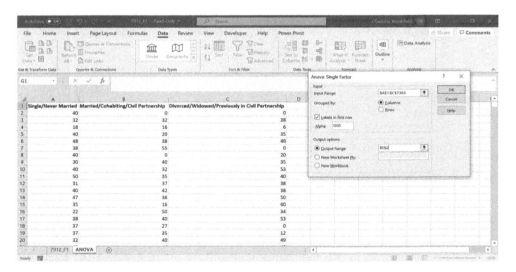

Figure 6.14 ANOVA test in Excel

The output for the ANOVA test will produce two tables. In the first table, you can see the mean value for each of the groups under investigation. This information is in the column labelled '**Average**'. In this example, the average number of hours worked by single/never married respondents was 30.75. Similarly, those respondents who were married/cohabiting or in a civil partnership worked on average 30.76 hours in the reference week. In comparison, those who were divorced/widowed or no longer in a civil partnership worked on average 28.97 hours in the reference week. In the output for the ANOVA test, it is necessary to look at the second table and the F statistic and the F critical statistic to determine whether there is a statistically significant difference in the value of the dependent variable between the groups (see Figure 6.15). If the F-value is greater than the F critical value, then the null hypothesis is rejected. This means that if the F-value is greater than the F critical value, we can conclude that there is a statistically significant difference in the mean values of the different groups under investigation. In this example, Figure 6.15 shows that the F-value is 6.79 and the F critical value is 3.00. As the F-value is greater than the F critical value, we can conclude that there is a statistically significant difference in the mean number of hours worked in the reference week according to the marital status of respondents. Alternatively, we can look at the p-value reported in the second table to deduce whether the difference between the groups is statistically significant. If the p-value is less than 0.05, then it can be concluded that there is a statistically significant difference between the groups. In the example in Figure 6.15, the p-value is 0.001 (less than 0.05) and, therefore, again we can conclude that the difference is statistically significant. This finding would be reported as (F=6.8, p<0.05).

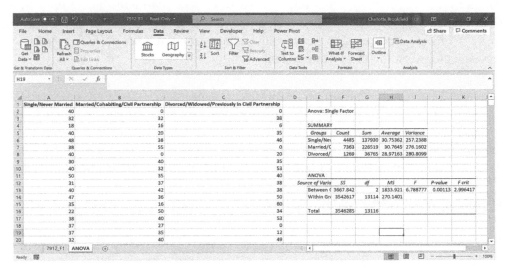

Figure 6.15 ANOVA output in Excel

6.6 Kruskal–Wallis Test in Excel

The Kruskal–Wallis test is used when you have more than two groups that you wish to compare; however, the data is not normally distributed for each group or your dependent variable contains ordinal level data. Similar to the Mann–Whitney U Test, the Kruskal–Wallis test cannot be calculated using the Analysis Toolpak in Excel. Instead, it is necessary to collate information and calculate the Kruskal–Wallis statistic yourself. Like the Mann–Whitney U Test, to begin the Kruskal–Wallis test it is necessary to rank the data.

The formula for the Kruskal–Wallis test is:

$$H = \left[\frac{12}{N(N+1)} \sum \frac{R^2}{n} \right] - 3(N+1)$$

where N is equal to the number of overall number of observations, n is equal to the number of observations in an individual group, and R is equal to the sum of the ranked data for each group. To calculate the Kruskal–Wallis statistic it is necessary to obtain the number of observations and the sum of the ranked data for the dependent variable for each group. Once you have this information, it can be substituted into the equation presented.

To begin, it is important to note how many participants from each group under investigation reported data for the dependent variable. This can be calculated using the Descriptive Statistics option (see Section 4.6). In this example, we have data on the total number of hours worked in the reference week for 4485 respondents who were 'Single/Never Married', for 7363 respondents who were 'Married/Cohabiting or in a Civil Partnership' and 1269 respondents who were 'Divorced/Widowed or previously in a Civil Partnership'. Overall, we have data on the total number of hours worked in the reference week for 13 117 respondents.

Secondly, it is necessary to rank the data from lowest to highest. In this example, this means that the participant across all three groups under exploration who worked the lowest number of hours in the reference week will be assigned the lowest rank, whereas the participant in the sample who worked the highest number of hours in the reference week will be assigned the highest rank. To rank the data, use the '=RANK. AVG' formula. The formula should look like this: RANK.AVG(Cell reference, Table

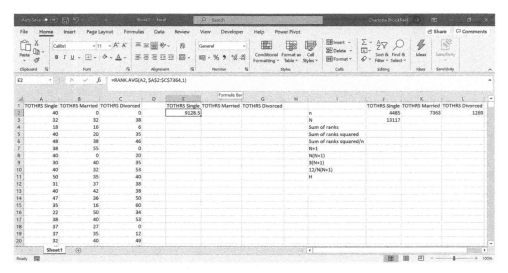

Figure 6.16 Ranking data in Excel

array, 1). In this example, the table array is cell A2 to cell C7364. '$' signs have been inserted around the table array so that the formula can be dragged and copied to the other cells, while locking in certain data. The '1' denotes that the cells should be sorted in ascending order (see Figure 6.16). This formula only needs to be dragged down for each group to the count for each group. For instance, as there are only 1269 respondents in 'Divorced/Widowed or previously in a Civil Partnership', the formula is only dragged down to cell G1270, whereas for 'Married/Cohabiting or in a Civil Partnership', it is dragged down to cell F7364.

Following this, you need to summate the rank scores for the dependent variable for each group (see Figure 6.17). In this example, this means adding the rank scores of those who are single, never married, those who are married, cohabiting or in a civil partnership, and those who are divorced, widowed or were previously in a civil partnership. For those who were 'Single/Never married' the sum of the rank scores was 29 548 145. For those who were 'Married/Cohabiting or in Civil Partnership' the sum of the rank scores was 48 668 756.5. For those who are 'Divorced/Widowed or were previously in a Civil Partnership' the sum of the rank scores was 7 817 501.5.

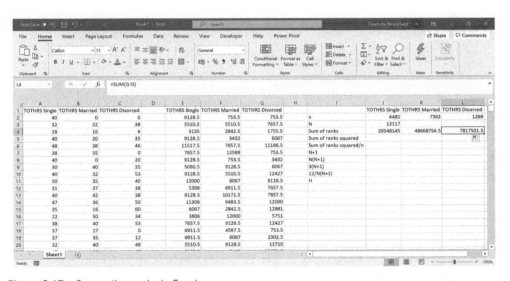

Figure 6.17 Summating ranks in Excel

This information can then be inserted into the formula as shown below:

$$H = \left[\frac{12}{N(N+1)} * \sum \frac{R^2}{n} \right] - 3(N+1)$$

$$= \left[\frac{12}{13117(13117+1)} * \left(\frac{29548145^2}{4485} + \frac{48668756.5^2}{7363} + \frac{7817501.5^2}{1269} \right) \right] - 3(13117+1)$$

To square the sum of the ranks for each group, you can use the '=POWER' formula in Excel. To square a number in Excel enter the following formula: '=POWER(Cell reference, 2)'. The cell reference is the number that you want to square, the 2 denotes the fact that you wish to square the number (see example in Figure 6.18).

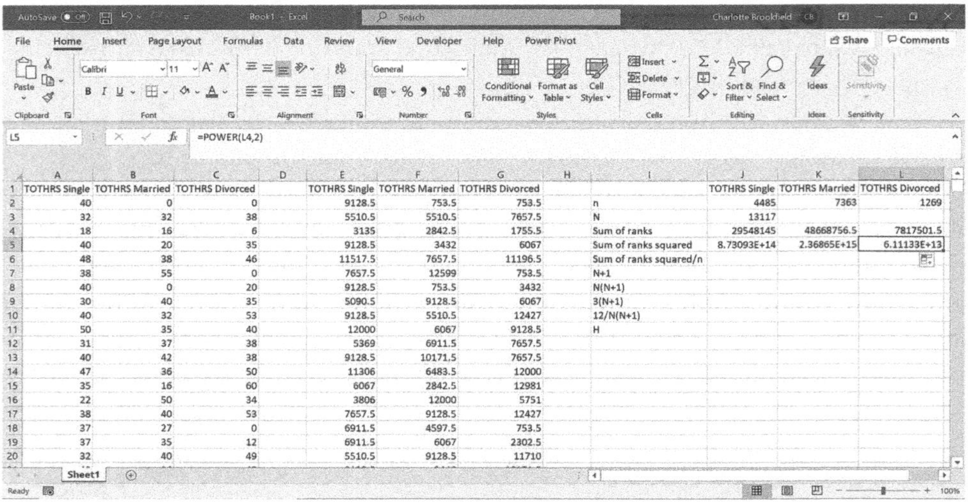

Figure 6.18 Squaring the sum of the ranks for each group in Excel

You now have all the information to calculate the H statistic for the Kruskal–Wallis test using the formula provided:

$$H = \left[\frac{12}{13117(13117+1)} * \left(\frac{29548145^2}{4485} + \frac{48668756.5^2}{7363} + \frac{7817501.5^2}{1269} \right) \right] - 3(13117+1)$$

$$= \left[\frac{12}{13117(13118)} * \left(\frac{29548145^2}{4485} + \frac{48668756.5^2}{7363} + \frac{7817501.5^2}{1269} \right) \right] - 3(13118)$$

$$= \left[\frac{12}{172068806} * \left(\frac{29548145^2}{4485} + \frac{48668756.5^2}{7363} + \frac{7817501.5^2}{1269} \right) \right] - 3934$$

$$= 39369.66 - 39354$$

$$= 15.66$$

This process is demonstrated in Figure 6.19.

The degrees of freedom need to be calculated in order to help deduce whether the Kruskal–Wallis statistic is statistically significant. The degrees of freedom are calculated by subtracting 1 from the number of groups. In the example used here, there are three groups so there are 2 degrees of freedom. The '=CHISQ.DIST.RT.' formula can be used to see whether the final figure is statistically significant. The formula should contain the Kruskal–Wallis statistic followed by the degrees of freedom. If the value is less than 0.05, then you can conclude that the difference between the groups is statistically significant and that the null hypothesis must be rejected. In the example used here (see Figure 6.20), the significance value is less than 0.05 and therefore we accept the alternative hypothesis and reject the null hypothesis. This would be reported as follows: there is a statistically significant difference in total hours worked by each group in the reference week (H=15.66, 2df, p<0.05).

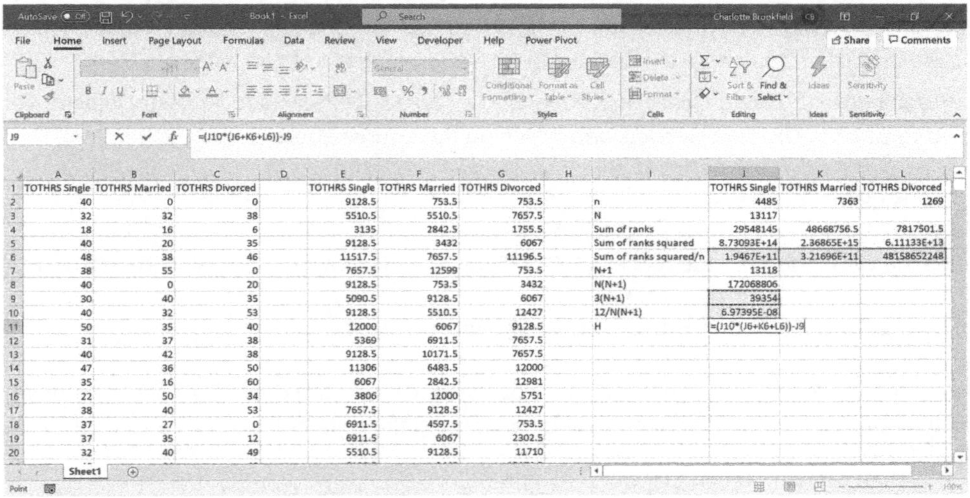

Figure 6.19 Calculating the H statistic in Excel

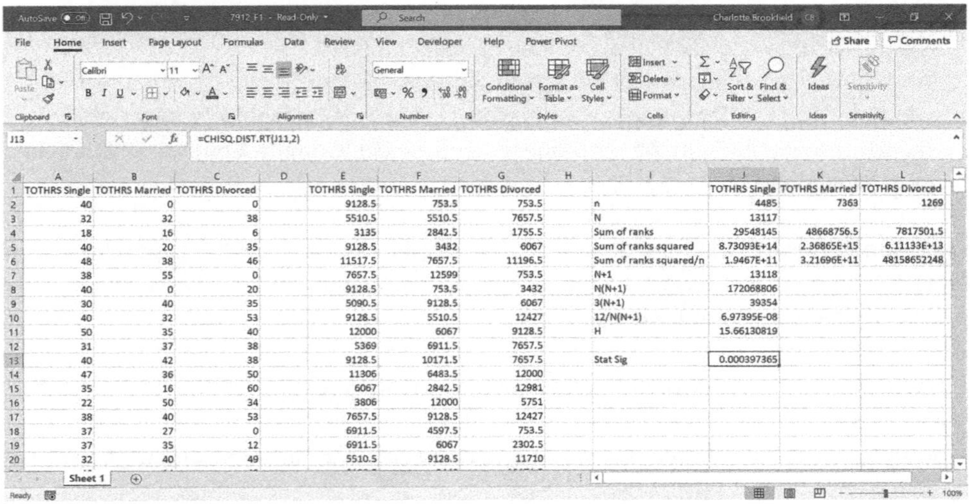

Figure 6.20 Testing for statistical significance for a Kruskal–Wallis test in Excel

Activity

Compare Mean Income and Expenditure

1. Download the Living Costs and Food Survey (2013) Unrestricted Access Dataset

The Living Costs and Food Survey (2013) Unrestricted Access Dataset is a subset of the original dataset and is simplified specifically for teaching. The Living Costs and Food Survey is the most significant consumer survey undertaken in the UK each year. It collates data on spending behaviours of households across the country. Those sampled for the survey are asked to keep a diary of expenditure for a period of two weeks.

To access the Living Costs and Food Survey (2013) Unrestricted Access Dataset, you need to visit the UK Data Service website using the address below:

www.ukdataservice.ac.uk

Once the webpage has loaded, select '**Get Data**' and in the search box type the following:

Living Costs and Food Survey (2013) unrestricted access dataset

Select the 2013 dataset. There are two ways to download the data. The first is by downloading the TAB file and the second is by accessing the data online. Both approaches are described here.

*   (Select the option to download the TAB file format of the data. Save the TAB data file on your computer. Then, open Excel and select '**File**' and '**Open**'. Browse for the TAB file, making sure that '**All Files**' are visible (the default is 'All Excel Files'). Once you have located the correct file, select '**Open**'. After this a series of windows will appear. Select '**Next**' to each of these and then choose '**Finish**'.
*   Alternatively, you can choose the option '**Access Online**'. This will open a new window. Click the '**Download**' button, which is towards the right in the top toolbar (floppy disc icon). From the drop-down menu, select '**Comma Separated Value**' and click '**Download**'.

In addition to downloading the data, it is often helpful to download the supporting documents for the dataset. These documents include information on how the variables in the dataset are measured and coded.

2. Compare the mean income across different government regions

Begin by creating histograms showing the income variable for three of the government regions:

Does the data appear to be normally distributed for each area?

....

Based on the histograms created, which test is most appropriate to use to compare the mean income between government regions?

....

3. Compare the mean expenditure across different government regions

What is the mean expenditure for each of the government regions explored?

....

Is there a statistically significant difference in expenditure between the government regions?

....

Further Reading

Haaker, M. 2019. *Little Quick Fix: Choose Your Statistical Test*. London: Sage.

Skills Checklist for Chapter 6

Use the checklist provided to track your learning and to highlight areas where you may need to do some additional reading.

	I can do this confidently	I could do this if I had a little more practice	I need more help with this
Determine which T-test or non-parametric test is most appropriate			
Run a T-test in Microsoft Excel			
Run a Mann–Whitney U Test in Microsoft Excel			

(Continued)

	I can do this confidently	I could do this if I had a little more practice	I need more help with this
Run an ANOVA test in Microsoft Excel			
Run a Kruskal–Wallis test in Microsoft Excel			

Ideas for Teachers/Instructors

Cookie Task

Divide students into groups and give each group a packet of a different brand of chocolate chip cookies. Students should 'calculate' the number of chocolate chips in each cookie in their group and record this information in an Excel worksheet. They should then use the data from each group to calculate whether there is a statistically significant difference in the mean number of chocolate chips in different brands of chocolate chip cookies. This activity is reported here:

Warner, B. and Rutledge, J. 1999. Checking the Chips Ahoy! Guarantee. *Chance* 12(1), pp. 10–14.

7

EXPLORING BIVARIATE RELATIONSHIPS: CORRELATION

Exploring the strength and direction of an association between two variables using Microsoft Excel

Colour Code for Chapter:
Amber
Study Skills:
Analysing and interpreting data
Research Methods Skills:
Bivariate analysis, Pearson's *r* correlation coefficient, Spearman's rho correlation coefficient
Microsoft Excel Skills:
Scatterplots, Correlation coefficients, Rank data
Datasets Used:
Living Costs and Food Survey, 2013: Unrestricted Access Teaching Dataset
Northern Ireland Police Recorded Injury Road Traffic Collision Data, 2015: Open Access

Visit **https://study.sagepub.com/brookfield** to download the datasets used in this chapter.

Chapter Outline

This chapter will give an overview of when and how to calculate correlation coefficients. Specifically, it will explain the underlying assumptions of Pearson's *r* correlation coefficient and Spearman's rho correlation coefficient. The chapter will include instructions on how to calculate both in Excel.

7.1 Introduction

Correlation is a form of bivariate statistical analysis which enables researchers to explore the strength and direction of a relationship or association between two variables. A correlation coefficient is a number which can be used to describe the relationship between two variables. It indicates whether, as the value of one variable increases or decreases, the value of the other variable also increases or decreases. Correlation coefficients can range between −1 and +1. A coefficient of −1 denotes a perfect negative relationship between the two variables and a coefficient of +1 denotes a perfect positive relationship between the two variables. A correlation coefficient of 0 indicates that there is no relationship between the two variables. Table 7.1 outlines how best to describe the relationship between variables, depending on the resultant correlation coefficient.

Table 7.1 Strength and direction of correlation coefficients

Correlation Coefficient	Description	Positive/Negative
−1	Perfect	Negative
−0.99 to −0.90	Very Strong	Negative
−0.89 to −0.70	Strong	Negative
−0.69 to −0.40	Modest	Negative
−0.39 to −0.20	Weak	Negative
−0.19 to −0.01	Very Weak	Negative
0	None	n/a
0.01 to 0.19	Very Weak	Positive
0.20 to 0.39	Weak	Positive
0.40 to 0.69	Modest	Positive
0.70 to 0.89	Strong	Positive
0.90 to 0.99	Very Strong	Positive
1	Perfect	Positive

There are two different correlation coefficients discussed in this chapter: the first is Pearson's *r* correlation coefficient and the second is Spearman's rho correlation coefficient.

Each section outlines the assumptions of the test and is followed by instructions on how to calculate the coefficients in Excel.

7.2 Pearson's r Correlation Coefficient

In order to calculate Pearson's r correlation coefficient, both the variables under investigation must be continuous level variables (see Section 4.2). A further assumption of Pearson's r correlation coefficient is that the data is normally distributed and that there is a linear association between the two variables, with no extreme outliers. Therefore, there are a number of steps that are necessary to undertake in order to investigate the data prior to calculating the correlation coefficient.

Remember Box 7.1

What is a linear relationship?

Linear relationship: Occurs when the two variables increase or decrease together at the same rate. On a graph, a linear relationship would appear as a diagonally straight line. An example of a linear relationship would be miles driven and fuel consumption.

7.3 Spearman's Rho Correlation Coefficient

Unlike Pearson's r correlation coefficient, Spearman's rho correlation coefficient can handle ordinal level data and deal with variables which are not normally distributed or do not have a linear relationship. The correlation coefficient in this instance is calculated using ranked data. The researcher begins with two variables that they are interested in, for instance height and weight. The data then needs to be ranked or, put simply, ordered from lowest to highest for each variable. Each participant in a dataset is given a rank for each variable under investigation. In this example, a participant would be given a rank for height and a rank for weight. This means that a rank of 1 would be assigned to both the shortest and the lightest person in the sample. Rather than using the raw data, Spearman's correlation coefficient uses the ranks to assess the strength and direction of the association between the two variables. For instance, it compares the ranks that individuals were assigned for their weight versus the ranks that they were assigned for their heights.

The decision tree in Figure 7.1 depicts the criteria used to determine whether it is most appropriate to calculate Pearson's r or Spearman's rho. Chapter 4 (see Section 4.5) explains how to deduce whether data is normally distributed. However, the instructions below outline how to create a scatterplot to see if the relationship between two variables is linear with no extreme outliers. Note that, if you do have extreme outliers, it may be worthwhile considering recoding your data to exclude these values (see Section 3.14).

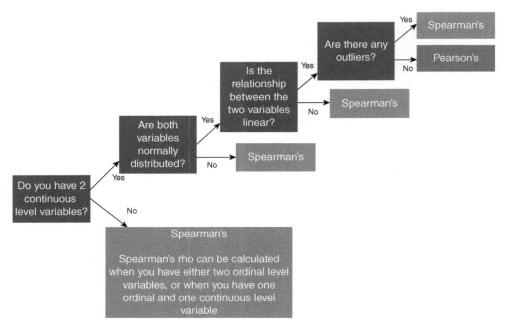

Figure 7.1 Decision tree – Pearson's *r* correlation coefficient or Spearman's rho correlation coefficient?

7.4 Scatterplots

A scatterplot enables a researcher to represent visually the relationship between two variables. A scatterplot displays values of the two variables under investigation simultaneously. Each dot on the scatterplot represents an individual. By reading down from the dot, researchers can see the value of x or the independent variable associated with a particular person in their sample, while reading across from the dot enables the researcher to see the value of y, or the dependent variable associated with a particular person or case in their sample. The scatterplot shows us whether there is a linear relationship between the two variables. It can also be used initially to assess the strength and direction of the relationship between two variables. Figure 7.2 shows three example scatterplots: one shows a perfect positive correlation, one shows a perfect negative correlation and the final example shows the typical scatterplot for situations where there is no relationship between the two variables.

Positive, Strong Correlation:

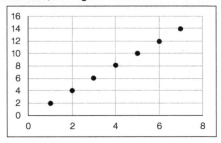

Negative, Strong Correlation:

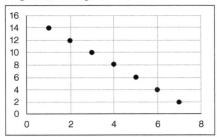

No Correlation:

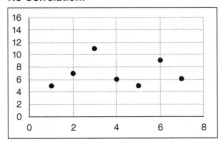

Figure 7.2   Scatterplots showing different strength correlations

7.5 Creating Scatterplots in Excel

To create a scatterplot in Excel, start by highlighting the columns that contain the data of interest. After this, select '**Insert**' from the top toolbar and under '**Charts**' select '**Scatter Chart**' (see Figure 7.3). Your scatterplot will appear straight away.

Insert > Charts > Scatter Chart

Excel will automatically plot the data closest to the left along the *x*-axis of the scatterplot. Meanwhile, Excel will plot the values of the second variable on the *y*-axis. Because of this, you may wish to copy and paste the variables of interest into a new worksheet in the order that is most suitable for your study.

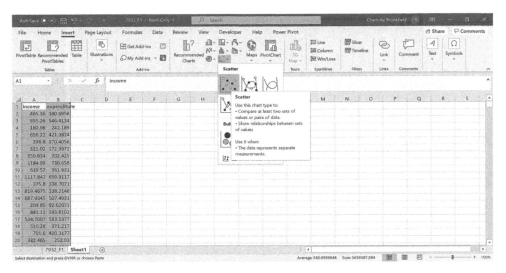

Figure 7.3   Inserting a scatterplot using Excel

Remember Box 7.2

Which is the x-axis and which is the y-axis?

X-axis: The x-axis is the horizontal axis and shows the values of the independent variable.

Y-axis: The y-axis is the vertical axis and shows the values of the dependent variable.

Once you have created your scatterplot, it is important to give it a title and to label the axis appropriately. This can be done by selecting '**Chart title**' and '**Axis titles**' under the 'Chart elements' drop-down menu. It is also important to add a line of best fit in order to comment on whether the relationship between the two variables is linear or not. To add a line of best fit, select '**Chart elements**' and then '**Trendline**', and then select '**Linear**' (see Figure 7.4). You may need to resize your graph to be able to clearly see the line of best fit.

In Excel 2016, you can also insert the equation of the line of best fit and the R^2 adjusted (the R^2 adjusted denotes what proportion of the variance in the dependent variable the independent variable explains; this will be revisited in Chapter 8). To add these features, under '**Chart Elements**', select '**Trendline**' and then click '**More Options…**'. This will open the '**Format Trendline**' menu and it is under this heading that you can select for the equation of the line to be displayed and the adjusted R² value.

The scatterplot can be used to deduce whether the relationship between the variables is linear. To calculate Pearson's *r* it is sufficient that the data trends towards linearity and is not obviously curving.

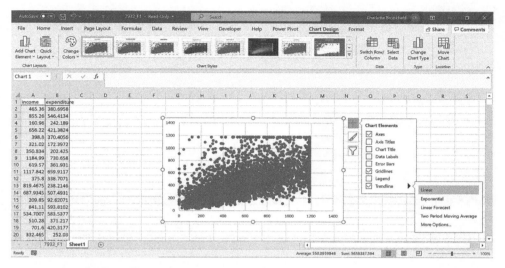

Figure 7.4 Inserting line of best fit on scatterplot using Excel

7.6 Pearson's r in Excel

There are two ways to calculate Pearson's *r* correlation coefficient in Excel. The first technique is menu driven, while the second approach involves entering a short formula. Both approaches will be explained.

In order to use the menu approach, the data in Excel needs to be rearranged so that the two variables of interest appear next to each other in the worksheet. The easiest way to do this is to copy and paste the two columns of data into a new worksheet. Once your data is formatted in adjacent columns, select '**Data**' from the top toolbar. Then, select '**Data Analysis**' and choose '**Correlation**' (see Figure 7.5). This will prompt a new window to open.

Data > Data Analysis > Correlation > OK

Select the columns of interest (tick '**Labels in First Row**' if applicable), then select where you would like the output to be presented and click **OK** (see Figure 7.6).

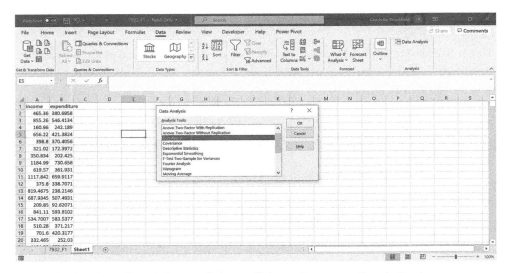

Figure 7.5 Calculating Pearson's *r* correlation coefficient using menu options in Excel

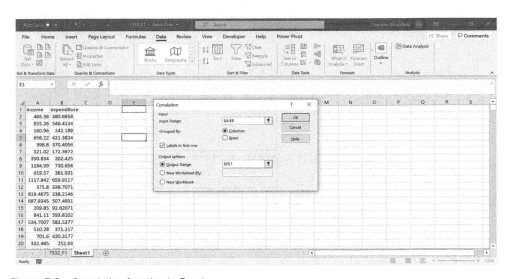

Figure 7.6 Correlation function in Excel

After this, a new table containing the correlation coefficient for the two variables will appear. In the example presented in Figure 7.7, Pearson's *r* correlation coefficient for the two variables **income** (gross normal weekly household income) and **expenditure** (total expenditure) from the Living Costs and Food Survey (2013) has been calculated. The coefficient is equal to 0.706. Using Table 7.1, we can conclude that there is a strong, positive relationship between gross normal weekly household income and total expenditure.

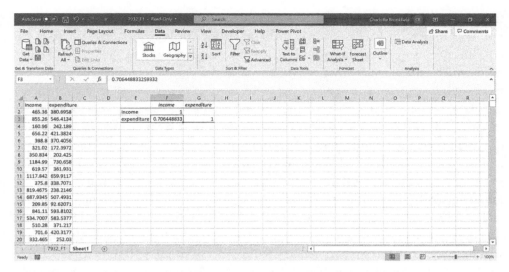

Figure 7.7 Pearson's *r* correlation coefficient between variables **income** and **expenditure**

An alternative and quicker approach to calculating Pearson's *r* correlation coefficient is by using the formula '=CORREL(Var1,Var2)'. This approach does not require the data to be formatted in adjacent cells. **Var 1** is replaced with the range of cells that contain data relating to one of your variables and **Var 2** is replaced with the range of cells that contain data relating to your second variable. In Figure 7.8, the correlation coefficient between **income** (gross normal weekly household income) and **expenditure** (total expenditure) is being calculated again, but this time using the correlation formula.

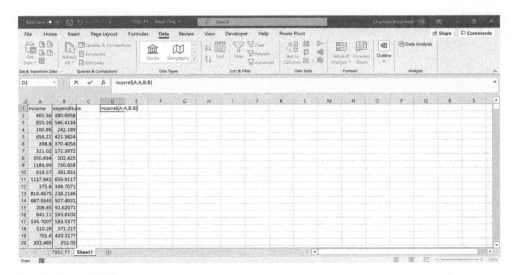

Figure 7.8 Correlation formula in Excel

In order to determine whether a correlation coefficient is statistically significant or not, it is important to identify whether the coefficient is higher or lower than the critical value using a significance table, like the one presented in Table 7.2. To determine which critical value you need to look at in the significance table, you need two pieces of information. The first of these is the number of degrees of freedom, which is calculated by subtracting 2 from the number of paired cases in your dataset. For instance, for the variables used in this example, 5144 respondents answered both questions. Therefore, the degrees of freedom would be 5142. The second piece of information you need is the significance level that you wish to use. Typically, in the social sciences, a significance level of 0.05 is used (see Section 5.1). The critical value can be found where the degrees of freedom and the significance level meet in the significance table. If the correlation coefficient is greater than the critical value, it can be deduced that the relationship between the two variables is statistically significant. Alternatively, significance calculators for correlation coefficients can be found online – these can be particularly helpful when you have larger samples. For the current example, the relationship between gross normal weekly household income and total expenditure is statistically significant at the 5% level.

Table 7.2 Critical values table: Pearson's r correlation coefficient

Sample Size	Degrees of Freedom	Significance Level 0.05
4	2	0.9900
5	3	0.9587
6	4	0.9172
7	5	0.8745
8	6	0.8343
9	7	0.7977
10	8	0.7646
11	9	0.7348
12	10	0.7079
13	11	0.6835
14	12	0.6614
15	13	0.6411
16	14	0.6226
17	15	0.6055
18	16	0.5897
19	17	0.5751
20	18	0.5614
21	19	0.5487
22	20	0.5368
23	21	0.5256

Sample Size	Degrees of Freedom	Significance Level 0.05
24	22	0.5151
25	23	0.5052
26	24	0.4958
27	25	0.4869
28	26	0.4785
29	27	0.4705
30	28	0.4629
40	38	0.4026
50	48	0.3610
60	58	0.3301
70	68	0.3060
80	78	0.2864
90	88	0.2702
100	98	0.2565

Alternatively, it is possible to return a significance value for a correlation cofficient in Excel if you use the regression option described in the following chapter. A regression model with two variables will return an R value which is the same as the correlation coefficient. The regression output also contains a significance value. If this is less than 0.05, then you can conclude that the relationship between the two variables under investigation is statistically significant.

7.7 Spearman's Rho in Excel

As Spearman's rho correlation coefficient explores the relationship between ranked data, the first step in the process of calculating the coefficient is ranking the data. To rank the data, it is necessary to use the RANK.AVG function.

It is important to note that Excel has two formulae to rank data: '=RANK.AVG' and '=RANK'. The difference is shown in Table 7.3. In the example there are six data points; however, for two observations the value of '2' has been recorded. When the data is ranked from lowest to highest using the '=RANK' function, both of these observations are ranked in second place and there is no third-place observation. When the data is ranked from lowest to highest using the '=RANK.AVG' function, these observations have been ranked as 2.5 and there is no second- or third-place rank. This is because Excel recognises that these two observations would form ranks 2 and 3, but as the values are identical it adds together the ranks and divides the result by the number of tied observations. In this instance the tied ranks are 2 and 3, which, summated, equal 5. There are two identical observations, which means that 5 must be divided by 2, leaving us with a rank value of 2.5.

Table 7.3 The difference between '=Rank' and '=Rank.Avg'

Raw Data	=Rank	=Rank.Avg
2	2	2.5
4	5	5
2	2	2.5
1	1	1
3	4	4
5	6	6

In the example in Figure 7.9, the RANK.AVG formula has been used to rank respondents' answers for the two variables **income** (gross normal weekly household income) and **expenditure** (total expenditure) from the Living Costs and Food Survey (2013). To use the RANK.AVG formula, begin by typing '=RANK.AVG(' and then insert the reference cell or the first cell that you wish to rank. In this case, it is cell A2. Following this, highlight the whole column. Again, in this example, the formula now looks like this: '=RANK.AVG(A2, A:A'. It is good practice to lock the column range by inserting '$' signs either side of the coordinates, for example $A:$A. After this, you need to tell Excel whether to rank the data in ascending or descending order. If you enter a '0' the data will be ranked in descending order, whereas if you enter '1' the data will be ranked in ascending order. For Spearman's rho correlation coefficient, the order does not matter; however, you must ensure that you order the two variables consistently (i.e. either both ascending or both descending). In the example in Figure 7.9, the data has been ranked in ascending order and the final formula appears as '=RANK.AVG(A2,$A:$A,1)'. Once the formula has been entered for the first cell in the column, it can be dragged down and copied to the remaining cells.

Figure 7.9 Rank.Avg formula in Excel

The respondents who reported having a gross normal weekly household income of £0 share the lowest rank. Equally, the respondents who reported having the lowest total expenditure (£30.53) share the lowest rank.

Once the data is ranked, Spearman's rho correlation coefficient can be calculated using either the menu-driven correlation option or the 'CORREL' formula (see description in Section 7.6).

As before with Pearson's *r* correlation coefficient, a significance table (see Table 7.4) can be used to determine whether the relationship is statistically significant.

Table 7.4   Critical values table: Spearman's rank

Sample Size	Degrees of Freedom	Significance Level 0.05
4	2	1.000
5	3	0.900
6	4	0.8286
7	5	0.7143
8	6	0.6429
9	7	0.6000
10	8	0.5636
11	9	0.5364
12	10	0.5035
13	11	0.4835
14	12	0.4637
15	13	0.4464
16	14	0.4294
17	15	0.4142
18	16	0.4014
19	17	0.3912
20	18	0.3805
21	19	0.3701
22	20	0.3608
23	21	0.3528
24	22	0.3443
25	23	0.3369
26	24	0.3306
27	25	0.3242
28	26	0.3180
29	27	0.3118
30	28	0.3063
40	38	0.2640
50	48	0.2353
60	58	0.2144

(Continued)

Table 7.4 (Continued)

Sample Size	Degrees of Freedom	Significance Level 0.05
70	68	0.1982
80	78	0.1852
90	88	0.1745
100	98	0.1654

Alternatively, additional steps can be taken in Excel to determine whether or not Spearman's rho correlation coefficient is statistically significant. The first step is to calculate the test value and the second is to calculate the resultant p-value. The formulae for these are outlined below:

$$\text{Test Statistic} = \text{rho} * \sqrt{\frac{(n-2)}{1-rho^2}}$$

p-value = TDIST(Test Statistic, df, 2)

where *rho* is equal to Spearman's rho correlation coefficient and *n* is equal to the number of paired observations. The degrees of freedom (df) can be calculated by subtracting 2 from the number of paired observations. The formula '=SQRT' can be used to find the square root of numbers in Excel and the formula '=POWER' can be used to square numbers (see Section 6.6). Figure 7.10 shows the process of calculating the test statistic and Figure 7.11 depicts the process of calculating the p-value in Excel. In Figure 7.11, the '2' at the end of the formula denotes that this is a two-tailed test and the hypothesis is not directional. The resultant p-value is less than 0.05 and therefore we can reject the null hypothesis.

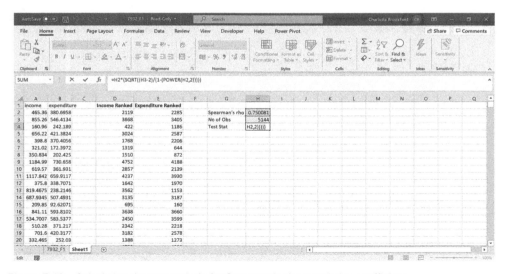

Figure 7.10 Calculating the test statistic for Spearman's rho correlation coefficient

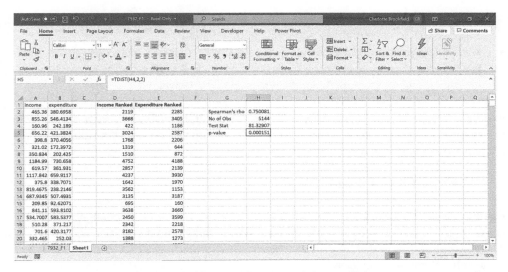

Figure 7.11 Calculating the p-value of Spearman's rho correlation coefficient

Calculate a Correlation Coefficient

1. Download the Northern Ireland Police Recorded Injury Road Traffic Collision Data (2015) Dataset

The Northern Ireland Police Recorded Injury Road Traffic Collision Data derives from information collected and stored by the Northern Ireland Police Service. This data is used to help inform government and police on road safety policies and initiatives. This activity uses the collisions data only. To access the Northern Ireland Police Recorded Injury Road Traffic Collision Data, you need to visit the UK Data Service website using the address below:

www.ukdataservice.ac.uk

Once the webpage has loaded, select '**Get Data**' and, in the search box, type the following:

Northern Ireland Police Recorded Injury Road Traffic Collision Data

Select the 2015 dataset. There are two ways to download the data. The first is by downloading the TAB file and the second is by accessing the data online. Both approaches are described here.

- Select the option to download the TAB file format of the data. Save the TAB data file on your computer. Then, open Excel and select '**File**' and '**Open**'. Browse for the TAB file, making sure that '**All Files**' are visible (the default is 'All Excel Files'). Once you

(Continued)

have located the correct file, select '**Open**'. After this a series of windows will appear. Select '**Next**' to each of these and then choose '**Finish**'.

- Alternatively, you can choose the option '**Access Online**'. This will open a new window. Click the '**Download**' button towards the right in the top toolbar (floppy disc icon). From the drop-down menu, select '**Comma Separated Value**'and click '**Download**'.

In addition to downloading the data, it is often helpful to download the supporting documents for the dataset. These documents include information on how the variables in the dataset are measured and coded.

2. Picking predictor variables

For this activity, you need to pick a variable to correlate with the variable **a_type**(collision severity). Pick a variable to correlate with collision severity from the list below:

a_veh   Number of vehicles

a_speed   Speed limit

a_cas   Number of causalities

3. Correlation coefficient

Use Excel to calculate the correlation coefficient between your variables.

Justify your choice of either Pearson's *r* correlation coefficient or Spearman's rho correlation coefficient.

Interpret your correlation coefficient – make sure you comment on the strength and the direction of the relationship between the variables.

....

....

....

....

Further Reading

MacInnes, J. 2019a. *Little Quick Fix: Know Your Variables*. London: Sage.

Wheelan, C. 2013. Correlation: How Does Netflix Know What Movies I Like? In: Wheelan, C. *Naked Statistics: Stripping the Dread from Data*. London: W.W.Norton, pp. 58–67.

Skills Checklist for Chapter 7

Use the checklist provided to track your learning and to highlight areas where you may need to do some additional reading.

	I can do this confidently	I could do this if I had a little more practice	I need more help with this
Identify whether data is normally distributed			
Create a scatterplot in Microsoft Excel			
Identify whether there is a linear relationship between two variables			
Determine whether it is most appropriate to calculate Pearson's r or Spearman's rho correlation coefficient			
Calculate Pearson's r in Microsoft Excel			
Calculate Spearman's rho in Microsoft Excel			
Interpret correlation coefficients			

Ideas for Teachers/Instructors

Strawberry Laces

Give each of your students a strawberry lace (or other long sweet). Ask the students to measure the lace and record this information. Then ask your students to take one bite of the lace and to re-measure it. Get them to repeat this process until they have eaten the entire lace. Then get them to create a scatterplot between the number of bites and the length of the lace. This will help demonstrate a negative relationship. As the number of bites increases, the length of the lace decreases. Some students may wish to go on to calculate the correlation coefficient for the data that they have collected.

Distance from Home

Ask your students to track how far away from their house they are every five minutes on their journey into the classroom. This can be done either 'live' or later in a classroom setting using the internet. Get the students to plot this data on a scatterplot. As the time increases, the distance from home also increases. This will help demonstrate a positive relationship. Some students may wish to go on to calculate the correlation coefficient for the data that they have collected.

8

EXPLORING MULTIVARIATE RELATIONSHIPS: LINEAR REGRESSION

Similar to correlation, but exploring how three or more variables relate to each other and investigating which variables can statistically significantly predict a particular outcome using Microsoft Excel

Colour Code for Chapter:
Red
Study Skills:
Analysing and interpreting data
Research Methods Skills:
Multivariate analysis, Linear regression
Microsoft Excel Skills:
Regression
Datasets Used:
Living Costs and Food Survey, 2013: Unrestricted Access Teaching Dataset
Northern Ireland Police Recorded Injury Road Traffic Collision Data, 2015: Open Access

Visit **https://study.sagepub.com/brookfield** to download the datasets used in this chapter.

Chapter Outline

This chapter introduces multivariate analysis. Specifically, it focuses on multiple linear regression and how this technique can be used to study more than two variables at once. Multiple linear regression is considered an extension of Pearson's *r* correlation coefficient (see Section 7.2).

8.1 Introduction

In some situations, it may be plausible that there is more than one variable which is associated with a dependent variable. In these situations, we need to employ multivariate analysis techniques to explore the impact of each of these variables on the dependent variable. One approach which can be adopted is multiple linear regression. Multiple linear regression is often described as an extension of Pearson's *r* correlation coefficient. Similar to correlation, regression also measures the strength and direction of the relationship between variables; however, multiple linear regression can also be used for forecasting and predicting values of a dependent variable for unobserved values of the independent variables. For instance, multiple linear regression could be used to predict the prices of properties. The size of a property, the number of bedrooms, distance from the city centre, size of the garden, and so on, could all help predict the price of the property. Therefore, in this example, our dependent variable would be property price and our predictor variables would be: size of property, number of bedrooms, distance from the city centre and size of the garden. Based on the data that we have on these variables, we can calculate the effect that each of these factors has on the final property price and use this information to create a formula that allows us to predict property prices. Care needs to be taken when extrapolating the formula beyond the survey sample and predicting values of the dependent variables. This is especially important if you believe your survey sample to be biased or unrepresentative in any way. The further you go beyond the realms of your model when predicting unobserved values, the less accurate the predictions will be.

For multiple linear regression analysis, the dependent variable is always a continuous level variable (see Chapter 4). The predictor variables can be either continuous or dichotomous categorical variables (categorical variables with two possible response options, e.g. yes/no; male/female).

8.2 Multiple Linear Regression in Excel

Fortunately, you can use the regression tool in Excel's '**Data Analysis ToolPak**' to run regression analysis quickly and easily. In this example, the Living Costs and Food

Survey, 2013: Unrestricted Access Teaching Dataset is used. Specifically, the dependent variable is total expenditure (**expenditure**) and the following variables are used in the model as predictors: income (**Income**); number of adults in the household (**G018r**) and number of children in the household (**G019r**). This means that the example will result in a formula that can be used to predict total expenditure based on income and the number of adults and number of children in a household. The resultant coefficients that are used to make this formula will also help us determine which of these predictor variables has the greatest impact on income. To assist with the analysis, all the variables of interest have been copied into a new worksheet.

To run the regression analysis, you begin by selecting the '**Data**' tab from the top toolbar menu. Then, select '**Data Analysis**'. This will open a new window with a menu of different tests. From this list, select '**Regression**' and click **OK** (see Figure 8.1).

Data > Data Analysis > Regression > OK

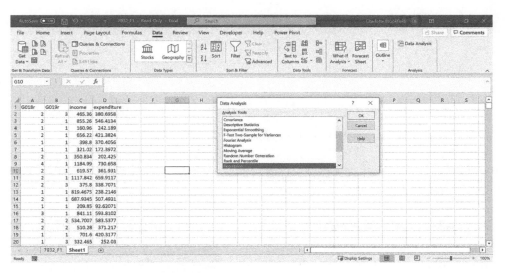

Figure 8.1   Linear regression in Excel

This will open a new window where you tell Excel the location of the variables that you wish to analyse in your worksheet (Figure 8.2). '**Input Y Range**' refers to the location of your dependent variable and '**Input X Range**' refers to the location of your predictor variables in your worksheet. In this example, '**Input Y Range**' refers to the cells containing data relating to expenditure (Column D) and '**Input X Range**' refers to the cells containing data relating to the number of adults in a household, the number of children in a household and the income of a household (Columns A, B and C). As has been done here, you should copy your data so that your predictor variables appear in adjacent cells. When entering your data, it is important that you do not select the whole column; instead you must select all the cells with data in them. In this example, this means that for the dependent variable, cells D1 to D5145 were selected and for the predictor variables, the range A1 to C5145 was selected. If the column headings are included in your selection, it is also necessary to select the '**Labels**' box (see Figure 8.2). The final step is deciding where to paste the output from the regression analysis. In this example (Figure 8.2) a location on the same worksheet has been selected. To run the test, click **OK**.

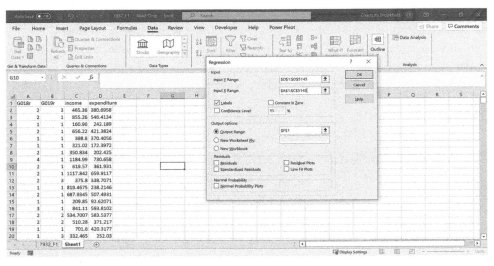

Figure 8.2   Selecting variables for linear regression in Excel

Your output should now appear. As shown in Figure 8.3, in total, Excel produces three tables of output for regression analysis.

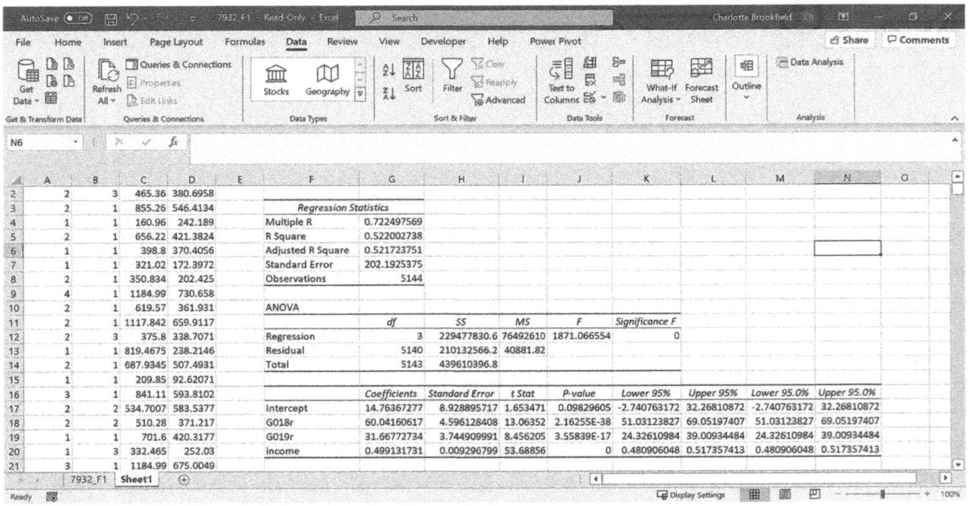

Figure 8.3   Linear regression output from Excel

The most important pieces of information from the first table (Regression Statistics) are the Number of observations, Multiple R value and the Adjusted R Square value. The number of observations tells you the number of valid cases included in the analysis. If there is missing data for any one of the variables being explored, a participant is excluded from the analysis. Therefore, when working with a dataset with high levels of missing data, the number of observations included in a regression analysis can decrease quickly. If you have a variable which has a high proportion of missing data, it is worth seriously considering whether it should be included in the model. In the example taken from the Living Costs and Food Survey, 2013: Unrestricted Access, all respondents have reported their total expenditure, income and the total number of adults and children in their household. As a result, data from all 5144 participants has been used in the regression model.

Remember Box 8.1

What is missing data?

Missing data refers to situations where a participant may decline responding, miss out a question or give an answer which cannot be understood or coded. Sensitive questions can lead to high levels of missing data. Often missing data is coded in a spreadsheet using a nonsensical value such as −99.

The Multiple R value is the same as Pearson's *r* correlation coefficient (see Chapter 7). This ranges from −1 to +1 and denotes the strength and direction of the relationship between the predictor variables and the dependent variable. In the example in Figure 8.3, the Multiple R value is 0.72, meaning that there is a strong, positive relationship between the predictor variables (income, number of children in household and number of adults in household) and the dependent variable (expenditure).

The Adjusted R Square value ranges between 0 and 1 and denotes the amount of variance in the dependent variable that the predictor variables in the regression model can explain. If the Adjusted R Square value equals 1, then the predictor variables explain all of the variance in the dependent variable. If the Adjusted R Square value equals 0, then the predictor variables explain none of the variance seen in the dependent variable. For instance, in Figure 8.3, the Adjusted R Square value is 0.52. This means that the predictor variables (income, number of children in household and number of adults in household) explain approximately half of the differences we see in total expenditure across the survey sample. It is common practice to multiply the Adjusted R Square value by 100 to convert the value into a percentage. Here, this would give us a percentage of 52%, meaning that we could conclude that our predictor variables explain 52% of the differences that we see among respondents in regard to total expenditure. The remaining 48% of variance is not explained by our model; it may be that other variables (which we may or may not have the data for) explain this remaining difference. For example, the number of cars owned per household may help us further predict differences in household expenditure. Unlike the R Square value (which is also in the Regression Statistics table), the Adjusted R Square value takes into account the number of variables that are included in the model and therefore is considered the more reliable measure of variance explained when you have more than one predictor variable in your model.

The second table of output (ANOVA) requires very little attention. The only thing that you need to report from this table is the Significance F-value. This will tell you whether or not your overall model is statistically significant. If the value is less than 0.05, it can be concluded that the model is statistically significant.

The final table of output explains the impact that each of the individual predictor variables has on the dependent variable. This allows you to deduce the extent to which one unit increase in each of the predictor variables impacts on the value of the dependent variable and also tells you whether the variables are statistically significant predictors of the dependent variable. In the example shown in Figure 8.3, we can see by looking at the p-value column that all the values are less than 0.05. This means that each of the variables is a statistically significant predictor of the total expenditure variable.

The next important thing to note in the final table is the value of the coefficients for each of the predictor variables. The intercept denotes the value of the dependent variable when all the predictor variables are equal to '0'. In this example, this means that the expenditure of a household with no income and no children or adults living there is £14.76. Each of the coefficient values tells you by how much the dependent variable increases or decreases. For example, for the predictor variable **G018r** (number of adults in the household) the coefficient in the table in Figure 8.3 is 60.04. This means that for every additional adult in the household, the total household expenditure increases from £14.76 by £60.04, making a total household expenditure of £74.80 for a household with one adult. For the variable **G019r** (number of children in the household), the coefficient is 31.67. This means that for every additional child in the household the value of the dependent variable, in this example expenditure, increases by £31.67, holding all other variables equal. The final predictor variable shown in Figure 8.3 is income. The coefficient for this variable is 0.499. This means that if we hold all other variables constant, for every additional £1 earned each week, then according to our regression model, household expenditure increases by 50p.

With this information, we can begin to predict values of our dependent variable for unobserved values of our predictor variables. For example, we can predict the total household expenditure for a household with two adults, four children and a household income of £452.98. We do this by multiplying these values by each of the coefficients and adding them together, along with the value of the intercept. As a formula, this would be written as $y = ax + bx + cx + d$, where a, b and c all refer to the coefficients for each of the predictor variables and d refers to the coefficient of the intercept. In our example, we would substitute the numbers into the formula as shown here:

$$y = (60.04 * 2) + (31.67 * 4) + (0.50 * 452.98) + 14.76$$
$$y = 120.08 + 126.68 + 226.49 + 14.76$$
$$y = 488.01$$

This means that for a household with two adults, four children and a household income of £452.98, we would predict the total weekly expenditure to be £488.01.

8.3 Using Categorical Variables in Regression Analysis

It is possible to use dichotomous categorical variables (categorical variables with two possible outcomes, e.g. yes or no) as predictor variables in a regression model. It is important that the dichotomous categorical variables are coded as '0' and '1'; therefore it may be necessary to do some recoding prior to undertaking the analysis (see Section 3.14.1).

Here, the variable **A172** (Internet Connection) is going to be added to the regression analysis model. Respondents could answer 'yes' or 'no' to having an internet connection. Respondents coded as '1' reported having an internet connection, while those coded as '2' did not have an internet connection. As shown in Figure 8.4, this variable has been recoded using a VLOOKUP function (see Section 3.7). Those who reported not having an internet connection were coded as a '0', while those who did have an internet connection were coded as a '1'.

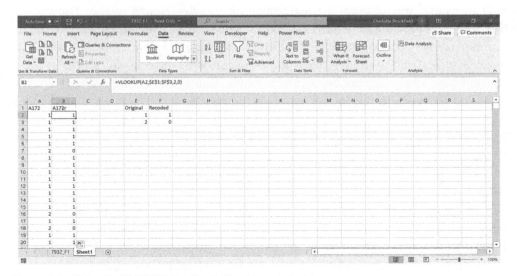

Figure 8.4 Using the VLOOKUP function in Excel to recode data

This recoded variable needs to be pasted next to the other predictor variables. It is important to remember that Excel will only run the regression analysis if the predictor variables are in adjacent columns. The data for the recoded variable should be pasted 'as values', otherwise it will copy the VLOOKUP formula only and not the numbers entered in the column. Figure 8.5 shows the predictor variables next to the dependent variable in Excel. The regression analysis is then undertaken in the same way as described above.

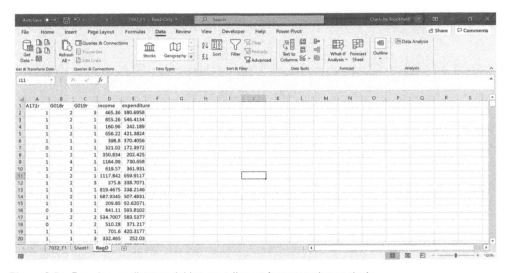

Figure 8.5 Ensuring predictor variables are adjacent for regression analysis

The output of the regression analysis is shown in Figure 8.6. Looking at the 'Regression Statistics' table, the Adjusted R Square value for this new model is 0.53. This means that the predictor variables in this model (income, number of children per household, number of adults per household and internet connection) explain 53% of the variance in expenditure among the sample. Comparing this with the previous model, we can see that by adding the variable **A172** (internet connection) to the model, we have increased the variance explained by 1%. As shown in Figure 8.6, all the variables included in the model are statistically significant predictors of household expenditure. The inclusion of the additional variable, **A172**, (internet connection) in this model has caused the coefficients for the other predictor variables to change; therefore, it is important to analyse and report each of the coefficients in turn. For the variable **G018r** (number of adults per household), the coefficient is now 55.10. This means that, holding all other variables in the model equal, each additional adult in the household leads to an increase in household expenditure of £55.10. For the variable **G109r** (number of children per household), the coefficient is 26.94. This means that, controlling for the other variables in the model, each additional child in the household leads to an increase in household expenditure of £26.94. Equally, for the income variable, the model predicts that for every additional £1 earnt, expenditure increases by 0.47 or 47p. For the recoded internet connection variable (**A172**), the coefficient is 76.38. This means that for those who have an internet connection (and are coded as 1), their total expenditure increases by £76.38.

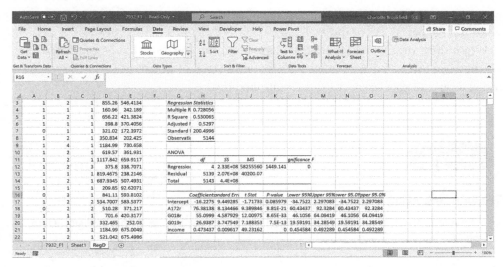

Figure 8.6 Regression analysis with a dichotomous categorical predictor variable in Excel

Using the coefficients and the intercept (–16.22), we can write an equation to allow us to predict household expenditure for unobserved values of the predictor variables. The equation is:

$$y = 55.10 * (G108r) + 26.94 * (G109r) + 0.47 * (Income) + 76.38 * (A172) - 16.22$$

Therefore, if we had a household with two adults, four children, an income of £452.98 and an internet connection, the household expenditure would be calculated in the following way:

$$y = (55.10 * 2) + (26.94 * 4) + (0.47 * 452.98) + (76.38 * 1) - 16.22$$
$$y = (110.20) + (107.76) + (212.90) + (76.38) - 16.22$$
$$y = 491.02$$

This means that, holding all other things constant, we can predict that a household with two adults, four children, an income of £452.98 and an internet connection, the household expenditure would be £491.02.

If we had a household with two adults, four children, an income of £452.98 and no internet connection, the household expenditure would be calculated in the following way:

$y = (55.10 * 2) + (26.94 * 4) + (0.47 * 452.98) + (76.38 * 0) - 16.22$

$y = (110.20) + (107.76) + (212.90) + (0) - 16.22$

$y = 414.64$

This means that, holding all other things constant, we can predict that a household with two adults, four children, an income of £452.98 and no internet connection, the household expenditure would be £414.64.

When substituting dichotomous variables into the equation, as demonstrated here, for the response coded as '1' the coefficient must be multiplied by 1. For the response coded as '0' the coefficient must be multiplied by 0.

Activity

Create a Regression Module

1. Download the Northern Ireland Police Recorded Injury Road Traffic Collision Data, 2015: Open Access Dataset

For this activity, you will need to download the Northern Ireland Police Recorded Injury Road Traffic Collision Data, 2015: Open Access. This dataset contains road collision data recorded by the Police Service of Northern Ireland.For this task, you will need to use the Excel workbook which is saved as 8021_F2.

To access the Northern Ireland Police Recorded Injury Road Traffic Collision Data, 2015: Open Access dataset, you need to visit the UK Data Service website using the address below:

www.ukdataservice.ac.uk

Once the webpage has loaded, select '**Get Data**' and, in the search box, type the following:

Northern Ireland Police Recorded Injury Road Traffic Collision Data, 2015: Open Access

Select the dataset. There are two ways to download the data. The first is by downloading the TAB file and the second is by accessing the data online. Both approaches are described here.

- Select the option to download the TAB file format of the data. Save the TAB data file on your computer. Then, open Excel and select '**File**' and '**Open**'. Browse for the TAB file, making sure that '**All Files**' are visible (the default is 'All Excel Files'). Once you have located the correct file, select '**Open**'. After this a series of windows will appear. Select '**Next**' to each of these and then choose '**Finish**'.

- Alternatively, you can choose the option '**Access Online**'. This will open a new wwindow. Click the '**Download**' button, towards the right in the top toolbar (floppy disc icon).From the drop-down menu, select '**Comma Separated Value**'and click '**Download**'.

In addition to downloading the data, it is often helpful to download the supporting documents for the dataset. These documents include information on how the variables in the dataset are measured and coded.

2.   Create a regression model

Begin by creating a regression model where the dependent variable is the number of casualties (**a_cas**) and the predictor variable is number of vehicles (**a_veh**).

Answer the following questions:

What percentage of the variance in the number of casualties from traffic collisions does the predictor variable (number of vehicles involved in a traffic collision) explain (the Adjusted R Square value)?

....

Is the predictor variable (number of vehicles involved in a traffic collision) a statistically significant predictor of the dependent variable (number of casualties in a traffic collision)?

....

Based on the data, for every extra vehicle involved in a traffic collision, how many additional casualties does the model predict there will be?

....

If there were 6 vehicles involved in a traffic collision, assuming all other variables were held constant, how many causalities would we predict?

....

If there were 15 vehicles involved in a traffic collision, assuming all other variables were held constant, how many causalities would we predict?

....

What other predictor variables would it be useful to include in our model (these do not necessarily have to be ones already reported in the Northern Ireland Police Injury Road Traffic Collision Data)?

....

Further Reading

Allison, P.D. 1999. *Multiple Regression: A Primer*. London: Sage.
MacInnes, J. 2019c. *Little Quick Fix: See Numbers in Data*. London: Sage.

Skills Checklist for Chapter 8

Use the checklist provided to track your learning and to highlight areas where you may need to do some additional reading.

	I can do this confidently	I could do this if I had a little more practice	I need more help with this
Run a regression analysis in Microsoft Excel			
Interpret the output of a regression analysis			
Recode a dichotomous categorical variable for regression analysis			
Run a regression analysis in Microsoft Excel with a dichotomous categorical predictor variable			

Ideas for Teachers/Instructors

Car Insurance Calculations

In order to explain the importance of looking at multiple variables at one time, use the example of how car insurance quotes are calculated. Ask students to consider what questions they might be asked when taking out car insurance. This will highlight how numerous variables, including age, number of years driving, number of accidents, and so on, are all used to determine the final car insurance quote.

9

BRINGING IT ALL TOGETHER: WRITING AND PRESENTING RESEARCH FOR DIFFERENT AUDIENCES

Presenting and visualising data for different audiences using Microsoft Excel

Colour Code for Chapter:
Green
Study Skills:
Analysing and interpreting data
Research Methods Skills:
Graphs, Charts, Infographics
Microsoft Excel Skills:
Pie chart, Bar chart, Line graph, Infographics, Maps
Datasets Used in this Chapter:
Death Registrations Summary Tables – England and Wales 2017
Opinions and Lifestyle Survey, Well-Being Module, January, February, April and May, 2015
Projections and Trajectory for the Number of Welsh Speakers Aged Three and Over, 2011 to 2050
Rough Sleepers by Local Authority 2018/19, Wales

Visit **https://study.sagepub.com/brookfield** to download the datasets used in this chapter.

Chapter Outline

This chapter will describe the ways you may choose to disseminate your research analysis for different audiences. Specifically, you will learn which graphs to use when presenting different levels of data (see Section 4.2). You will also begin to consider how to make your data visually appealing to a wider audience and the importance of clear graphs, tables and images in conveying key messages from social science research.

9.1 Introduction

Data visualisation is the process of formatting large amounts of data into an accessible, visually effective format. This can help audiences to identify quickly and easily the main 'headlines' behind the data. Effective use of tables, graphs, charts, maps, info-graphics and icons can help you tell a story with your data. It is important to consider carefully the most appropriate way to display your data. De Vries (2019) highlights examples of how graphics can be produced to convey a particular message. This can lead the audience to draw inaccurate conclusions.

9.2 Research Posters

You may be asked to present findings of a research project as a poster. Creating an eye-catching poster that conveys sufficient information in a concise manner can be a challenge. It is important to ensure that you include all the key points and enough detail for others to understand what you did to obtain your research findings. However, at the same time, you want your poster to be visually pleasing and not overcrowded.

Before starting your poster, check with the event organiser, or the person responsible for printing and displaying the posters, what size your poster needs to be. It is important that you set your document to the correct size before you start making your poster, otherwise you may find that graphics are pixelated or cramped when your final poster is printed.

When designing your poster, think about what key messages you need to convey. You will only have limited space and you do not want to overcrowd the page; therefore, it is important to prioritise the most essential and key messages. In addition to this, bear in mind that English is read from left to right. As such, see your poster as a storyboard where the early stages of your research project (such as your literature review) are presented on the left and the later parts of your research are presented on the right (such as your main findings). Make titles and subheadings on your poster bold and/or in a bigger font – again this will help the reader.

For research posters, less is more! Too much text can make your poster very unappealing and less eyecatching. Remember that the aim of a research poster is to catch someone's attention when they walk past. They need to be able to see and absorb key messages quickly and easily. Therefore, use clear fonts that are easy to read and use an appropriate font size that will be visible to most people when they are standing approximately 1 metre away.

Graphs, tables and infographics can be a very effective way of displaying a lot of data in a limited space on a research poster. Consider how you can incorporate these in order to convey important information about your research.

9.3 Research Presentations

In some instances, you may be required to present the findings from your research to an audience. Usually this will be a presentation followed by questions from the audience. Presentations can seem somewhat daunting; however, many find the experience to be fulfilling and rewarding. Presenting your work as part of your university studies can also be very good preparation for employment and can help you effectively demonstrate your communication skills to potential employers.

Practice is key to a good presentation. Ensure that you practise your presentation to yourself both in your head and aloud. It can also be advantageous to have trial runs of your presentation with friends or family. Ask these people to give you constructive feedback and to point out which parts of the presentation were particularly clear and which parts needed more work. Practising your presentation with groups who are not necessarily familiar with your research project can help you to consider the clearest and most concise way to explain your project and will encourage you to remember to provide definitions for key words and to avoid jargon. It is also important when you are practising your presentation to time yourself; this will help you gauge whether your presentation is likely to fill your allocated time. Often people find that they talk slightly quicker when presenting to others; therefore it can be useful when you are planning a presentation to note points where you could expand or elaborate if time permits. Equally, it may be advantageous to include a couple of additional slides at the end of your presentation which you can present if time allows; however, they are not imperative to the presentation if they are not addressed. Particularly if you are nervous, it may be a good idea to take a bottle of water to a presentation. Just knowing that you have water to hand can eliminate any fear that your throat will become dry. Do not be afraid to drink water during the presentation; this can calm your nerves and give you time to think through an answer to a question without rushing to the first thing that comes into your head. It can also be sensible to save a copy of your presentation in multiple places and email a copy of it to yourself. Again, this can remove the fear of losing or not being able to access your presentation, and help alleviate any nerves.

9.3.1 Structuring your presentation

Like a written piece of work, it is important that you carefully consider how you will structure a presentation. You need to ensure that your presentation has a clear introduction and a clear conclusion and that the main elements of the presentation are signposted. At the start of the presentation it is important to introduce yourself and your research project. This should be followed by a brief summary of what you are planning to cover in your presentation. If your work is part of a bigger project it may also be worth explaining this and noting the areas that will not be discussed in your presentation. At the start of a presentation, it can also be useful to share a fact, statistic or current story that underscores the necessity of your research and really draws the reader in. This technique can help build anticipation and excitement of what is to come. You will then move on to the key ideas or messages of your presentation. It can be helpful to return periodically to your outline for the presentation so that the audience can keep track. It is important to restrict the number of key messages or parts that you have in an individual presentation. The audience will only be able to retain or concentrate on a few ideas; therefore, while it can seem frustrating not to include certain aspects of your research in your presentation, it is useful when planning your presentation to consider which elements will be of most interest to your audience and are truly imperative to the message which you wish to convey. Towards the end of your presentation you need to summarise the key messages and the implications of these. For instance, you may want to talk about your intended next steps with the research or possible future research activities. It is also customary to thank the audience for their attention and invite any questions from them. The question part of the presentation can be the section that people are most apprehensive about, as you are unable to plan for this in quite the same way as the rest of the presentation. However, questions posed by the audience usually aim to seek clarification on a point raised in the presentation or to probe a little further on something that has been mentioned. It is important to listen carefully to any questions posed and to make good eye contact with the person asking the question. If this person is softly spoken it can be advantageous to repeat the question so that the rest of the room are aware of what you are about to discuss. Equally, repeating the question in this way can give you a couple more seconds to think of an appropriate response. When answering questions, it is also okay not to know the answer!

How Do You Respond When You Don't Know the Answer to a Question?

'That is a very interesting point that I have not considered yet.'

'I have not come across that, but I will make a note to look at it further.'

'For this project, that has not come up yet, but it is certainly worth my considering or looking into it.'

'That is a helpful suggestion/comment and not something I have considered but will endeavour to discuss with my supervisor in more detail.'

'Unfortunately, I don't really have a clear or definitive answer for that question at the moment, but I do know that...'

Sometimes you can even use questions as an opportunity to get other audience members involved, for example you could say: 'In my own experience, I have not come across that issue. What about other people in the room?'

9.3.2 Visual aids

Visual aids can be really helpful when presenting, but it is important that they are used effectively; otherwise they can become a distraction and deter the audience from the key messages in your presentation. When using visual aids such as Microsoft PowerPoint, avoid the temptation to use lots of animations, graphics and colours. Instead think carefully about colour choices, and ensure text is in a clear font and an appropriate size that is easy to read. Try to avoid using too much text and instead stick to short, key messages. It can also be helpful to use graphics including graphs, charts and tables to summarise information and display data.

Table 9.1 outlines some of the 'dos and don'ts' when creating presentations in Microsoft PowerPoint. It can also be a useful activity to reflect on what annoys you or, equally, what you find more appealing when watching other people present.

Table 9.1 Dos and Don'ts when creating presentations in Microsoft PowerPoint

Dos	Don'ts
Choose a text font and size that are clear and easy to read	Use fonts that are hard to read or are too small
Use bullet points or short sentences to summarise key messages	Include long paragraphs of text
Use tables, diagrams and charts to summarise important information	Make the slides too full or busy – if necessary, use multiple slides to convey one key point
Use images. Make sure that the images are relevant and that you explicitly refer to them in your presentation	Include too many images or bright, clashing colours, and avoid using animations

9.4 Research Reports and Dissertations

Dissertations and research reports are often more extended pieces of writing. Typically, these will be divided into chapters or sections. These chapters or sections may consist of: Introduction; Literature Review; Methods; Data Analysis; Discussion; and Conclusion. Each institution or organisation will have its own regulations and guidance on how to structure dissertations and research projects and word counts. It is important that you familiarise yourself with these before you start writing.

Table 9.2 outlines the aims of each chapter or section that you would need to include in a research report or dissertation.

Table 9.2 Chapters or sections included in a dissertation or research report

Chapter/Section	Aim
Introduction	Draw the reader in
	Outline the research problem
	Signpost the structure for the rest of the report/dissertation (e.g. Chapter 2 explores existing research in this area)
Literature Review	Critically engages with existing relevant literature
	Synthesises existing relevant literature
	Identifies gaps in the existing relevant literature
	Identifies the limitations of the existing relevant literature
	Leads to the development of research questions
Methods	Outlines the data collection method and analysis techniques used in the study
	Provides clear justification for the chosen method and analysis
	Critically discusses the strengths and limitations of the chosen method and analysis
	Considers how the researcher's own positionality may have impacted on the data collection and analysis
Analysis	Presents the data from the study
Discussion	Discusses the findings from the study critically
	Discusses the findings from the study in relation to existing relevant literature
	Contextualises the findings
Conclusion	Summarises the research and key findings
	Considers the implications of the findings on policy and practice
	Makes recommendations based on the findings
	Discusses the limitations of the research
	Suggests ideas for further research

As with all academic work, it is important to reference properly any sources used in your research report or dissertation. As discussed in Section 3.4, it is important that you are familiar with your institution's or organisation's preferred referencing style.

Normally, before the main body of the report or dissertation you will include an abstract. The abstract should provide a concise summary of the research that you have undertaken. Equally, after the main body of the report or the dissertation, it is good practice to include appendices. These will include relevant information that you have used during the data collection and analysis process. For example, you may choose to include a copy of your survey tool or interview guide.

9.5 Formatting Tables

It is often necessary to present data in tables as part of a research project. It is important that tables are concise and clear to the reader. There are some general rules to follow when creating tables:

- Give your table a clear and concise title. Who/what, where and when does the data refer to?
- Number tables clearly: Table 1, Table 2, etc.
- Avoid vertical lines in tables.
- State the unit of measurement in row and column headings (count, percentages, cm, etc.).
- If you are reporting statistical significance in your table, use asterisks and a key to denote this (*$p<0.05$, **$p<0.01$, ***$p<0.001$).
- Report the total number of valid cases at the bottom of the table ($n=1463$).
- If applicable, cite the source of the data at the bottom of the table.
- It may be important to consider changing the direction of the text in the table to ensure that it is all in view for the reader.

9.6 Formatting Charts and Graphs

As with tables, there are some important things to remember to include when you are presenting your research in a chart or graph. These include the following:

- Give your chart or graph a clear and concise title. Who/what, where and when does the data refer to?
- Number charts and graphs: Figure 1, Figure 2, etc.
- Label graph axes.
- State the unit of measurement alongside axis titles (count, percentage, cm, etc.).
- If applicable, cite the source of the data at the bottom of the graph or chart.

9.7 Charts and Graphs in Excel

9.7.1 Bar charts in Excel

Ordinal level data is often most effectively presented in bar charts. In these situations, the vertical bars on the chart indicate the percentage or frequency of different response categories. The tallest vertical bar represents the mode response.

To create a bar chart using Excel, begin by creating a frequency table for the variable of interest. To create the frequency table, you will need to use the Countif function (see Section 4.7). The frequency table will outline the number of respondents who gave a particular response category. In this example, the variable **QHealthr** (How is your health in general?) from the Opinions and Lifestyle Survey, Well-Being Module, April and May 2015, is used. The possible response options for this variable were: 'Very Good', 'Good', 'Fair', 'Bad' and 'Very Bad'. The Countif function was used to find that 750 people responded 'Very Good', 791 responded 'Good', 359 responded 'Fair', 107 responded 'Bad' and a further 37 responded 'Very Bad'. This is shown in Figure 9.1.

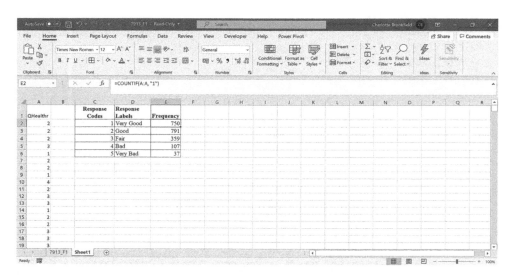

Figure 9.1 Frequency table for variable **QHealthr** in Excel

To visualise this data using Excel, begin by highlighting the 'Response Labels' and 'Frequency' columns in your frequency table. Select '**Insert**' from the top toolbar and then select '**Recommended Charts**'; this will open a new window. In the new window, select the tab at the top labelled '**All Charts**'. Then, from the list on the left, select '**Column**' and the '**Clustered Column**' chart. Click **OK** and your graph will appear. You can then edit your graph in various ways (see Figure 9.2).

Insert > Recommended Charts > All charts > Column charts > Clustered column chart > OK

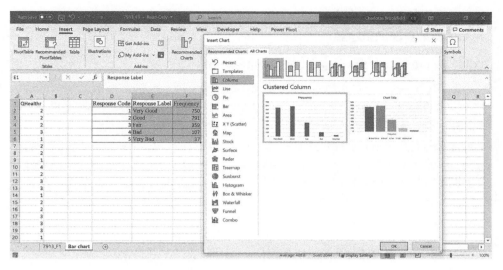

Figure 9.2 Inserting a bar chart in Excel

It may be more useful to format your graph so that the Y-axis displays the percentage of people who responded in a particular way. To do this, you need to add an extra column to your frequency table, with the heading 'Percentage' (as shown in Figure 9.3). To calculate the percentage of survey participants that gave each response, divide the frequency for each response by the total number of valid responses and multiply the answer by 100.

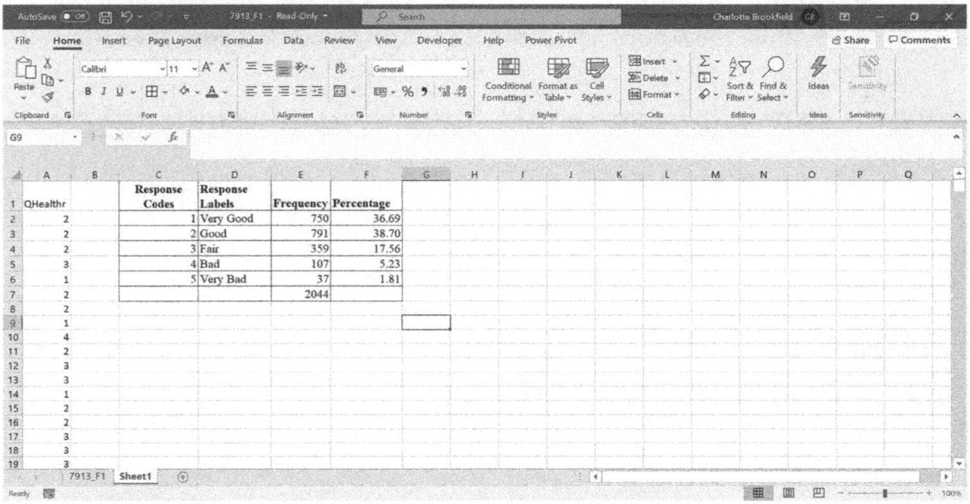

Figure 9.3 Calculating percentages in Excel

Once you have calculated the percentages, the process of inserting the bar graph is the same as before.

─Remember Box 9.1─

What do the x- and y-axis on a bar graph show?

X-axis: The x-axis on a bar graph shows the different values that the variable under investigation can take. Excel always uses the first column of data highlighted in a worksheet as the x-axis for a graph.

Y-axis: The y-axis on a bar graph shows the frequency or percentage of respondents who answered in a particular way. Excel always uses the second column of data highlighted in a worksheet as the y-axis for a graph.

9.7.2 Clustered bar charts in Excel

Clustered or stacked bar charts enable researchers to display visually the relationship between two variables (the independent and dependent variable). For instance, when looking at the Opinions and Lifestyle Survey, Well-Being Module, April and May 2015, it is possible to create a clustered bar chart to compare and contrast the self-reported quality of health of respondents (**QHealthr**) depending on their marital status (**martstat3**).

To create a clustered bar chart in Excel, it is necessary to have the data organised in a table or crosstabulation, with the independent variable along the side and the dependent variable along the top (see Section 5.4). Once the data is highlighted, select '**Insert**', '**Recommended Charts**' and choose '**All Charts**' from the tab at the top. Select '**Column**' from the list on the left and then '**Clustered Column**' (see Figure 9.4).

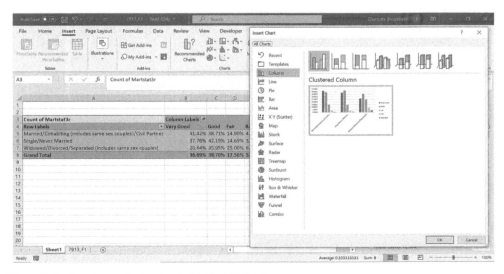

Figure 9.4   Creating a clustered column chart in Excel

Click **OK** and your clustered bar graph will appear. You can then edit your graph in various ways.

Insert > Recommended Charts > All Charts > Column > Clustered Column > OK

9.7.3 Pie charts in Excel

Nominal level data is often presented in pie charts. In these situations, the segments of pie indicate the percentage of a particular response category. Each segment is colour coded to represent a different response category. The largest segment of the pie chart represents the mode response. If every participant in a study chose a particular response option, the pie would be shaded completely in one colour. If half of the participants in a study chose a particular response category, 50% of the pie chart would be shaded in one particular colour to denote this.

To create a pie chart in Excel, it is necessary first to create a frequency table using the Countif function (see Section 4.7). In this example, the variable **Martstat3r** (marital status) from the Opinions and Lifestyle Survey, Well-Being Module, April and May 2015, has been used to create a pie chart. The frequency table shows that 1069 respondents reported being married, cohabiting or being in a civil partnership (see Figure 9.5). A further 430 participants reported being single, while 549 described their marital status as widowed, divorced or separated.

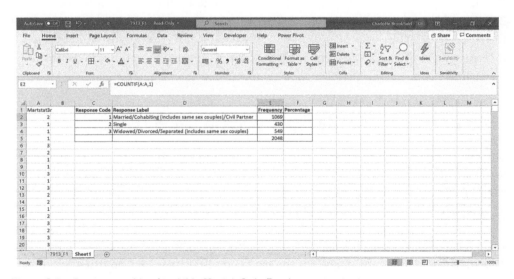

Figure 9.5   Frequency table of variable **Martsta3r** in Excel

To create the pie chart, highlight the frequency table. Then, select '**Insert**' from the top toolbar and click '**Recommended Charts**'. This will open a new window. At the top of this new window, select the option '**All Charts**' and then choose '**Pie**'. Click **OK** to insert the chart (see Figure 9.6). You can then edit your pie chart in various ways.

Insert > Recommended Charts > All Charts > Pie > OK

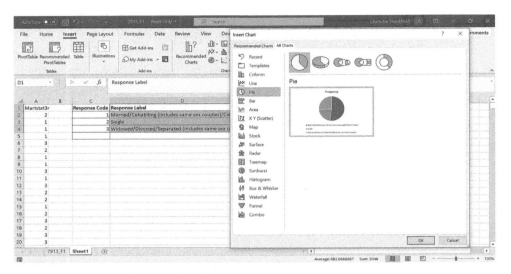

Figure 9.6   Inserting a pie chart in Excel

The use of pie charts to display social science data is, however, contested (Tufte, 2001). For instance, Tufte (2001:178) argues that pie charts are poor representations of data. The lack of scale in a pie chart and the cognitive burden of interpreting the size of different segments mean that inaccurate conclusions may be easily drawn.

9.7.4 Line graphs in Excel

Line graphs can be particularly effective at demonstrating change over time. For instance, line graphs are often used to show changes in the size of populations. In the example shared here, trajectory data is used to graph the expected number of people in Wales over the age of 3 who will be Welsh speakers by the year 2050.

To create a line graph, begin by ensuring your independent variable (in this example, year) is on the left and your dependent variable is on the right. Once the data is formatted in your worksheet, highlight the data and select '**Insert**' from the top toolbar. Under the '**Recommended Charts**' menu, select '**All Charts**' and choose '**Line**'. Your graph should then appear (see Figure 9.7). Give your line graph an appropriate name and ensure that each axis is labelled.

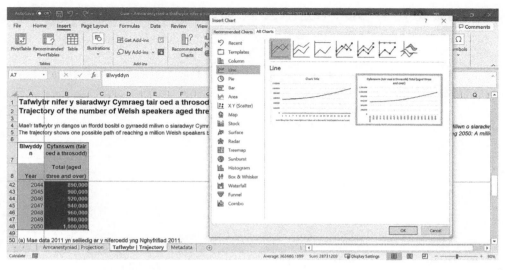

Figure 9.7 Inserting a line graph in Excel

9.8 Infographics and Maps

Infographics can help you tell a story with data. They can assist in making presentations or posters more eye catching and can be an effective way to simplify and display data, particularly if you are presenting to non-expert audiences.

9.8.1 People graphs in Excel

People graphs in Excel can be used to visualise the proportion of participants who gave a particular response. They can be particularly helpful at displaying the findings of bivariate analysis. In the example presented here, a people graph is used to demonstrate the death rate of each age group according to an extract from the *ONS Death Registrations Summary Tables – England and Wales 2017* (Office for National Statistics, 2018).

To create a people graph, you need to ensure that the '**People Graph**' add-in is installed on your version of Excel. The People Graph option is available under the '**Insert**' tab. If the option does not appear, select '**Get Add-Ins**' and search for '**People Graph**'. Select '**Add**' to install the People Graph' option.

To insert a people graph, go to the '**Insert**' tab and select '**People Graph**' (see Figure 9.8). This will open a template People Graph with fictious data.

Insert > People Graph

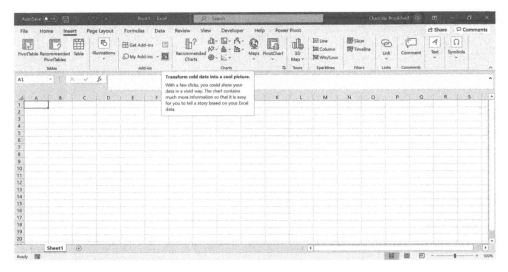

Figure 9.8   Inserting a people graph in Excel

The People Graph can only display a maximum of 15 rows of data at a time. Because of this, in the example used here the data has been recoded from the original 22 age brackets down to 5 age brackets.

Once the People Graph has opened, you will notice two menu options in the top right corner. These are '**Data**' and '**Settings**'. To begin, click '**Data**'. In this box, insert an appropriate title for your graph; in this example, the title 'Deaths according to age category' has been used. Next, click '**Select Data**' and highlight the columns of data that you wish to include in your graph. The first column should be a categorical

Figure 9.9   A people graph in Excel

variable and the second column should be a continuous variable. The information in the second column is used to determine how many people should be shaded in on your graph. In Figure 9.9, the new title has been inserted and the data selected.

After this, you can use the **Settings** option to change the look of your graph. For example, you can change the icons on your graph, or the colours used. It may also be advantageous to add a text box with axis labels. For instance, it would be beneficial in the example used here to make it clear that the numbers on the left are actually percentages.

There is an alternative way to create 'People Graphs' where you can have more than 15 rows and have a much greater variety of icons to choose from. However, the process takes slightly longer. This second method involves highlighting the data and selecting the '**Insert**' tab. Then choose '**2-D Clustered Bar Chart**' (see Figure 9.10). This will create a bar chart of your data.

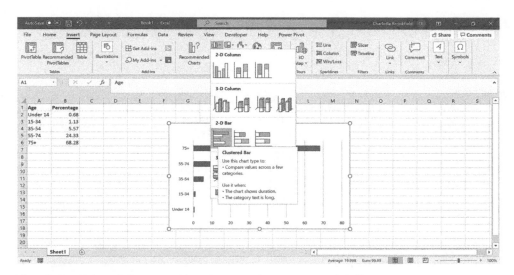

Figure 9.10 Using a 2-D clustered bar chart to make a people graph in Excel

Right click one of the bars on the graph and select the option **Format Data Series**. Select the **Fill** option from the 'Format Data Series' menu and change the current selection from '**Automatic**' to '**Picture or texture fill**'. Scroll down to the **Picture source** option and select '**Insert**'. This will then give you a choice of whether you would like to insert a picture that you have saved on your computer, a picture from the internet or an icon. In the example in Figure 9.11 an icon has been used.

Once you have selected the most appropriate graphic for your graph, you may notice that your pictures appear to be stretched on your graph. To correct this, scroll further down the '**Format Data Series**' menu and select '**Stack**' (see Figure 9.12).

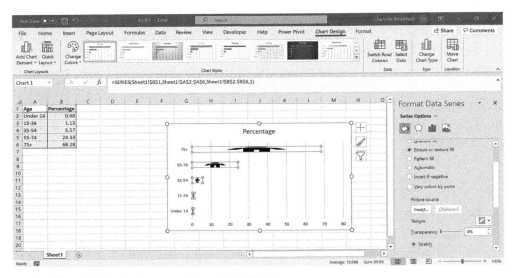

Figure 9.11 Inserting icons on people graphs in Excel

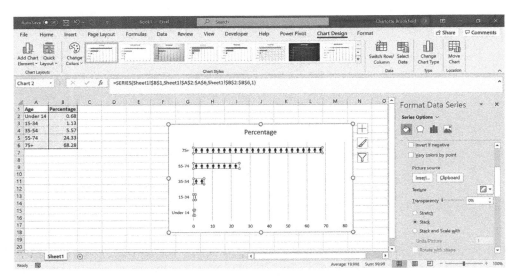

Figure 9.12 Stacking images for people graphs in Excel

If you wish, you can remove the gridlines from your graph. Remember to add an appropriate title and axis labels.

You can use different icons for different bars in the chart. For instance, if you wanted to compare the death rate at different age ranges for males and females, you could use different icons (see Figure 9.13).

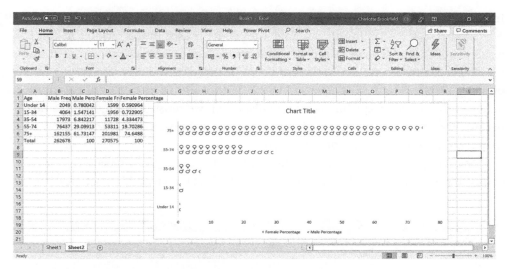

Figure 9.13 Using different icons in people graphs in Excel

9.8.2 Interactive charts and graphs in Excel

You can also make your charts interactive. This can be helpful when presenting them online or even in a presentation. To make your graph or chart interactive, begin by copying and pasting your frequency table into a new worksheet. Then paste another copy of your frequency table below. It is important to use the Paste Special option and select '**Paste Values**'. Then, in the second frequency table, delete the data, keeping just the column and row headings (see Figure 9.14).

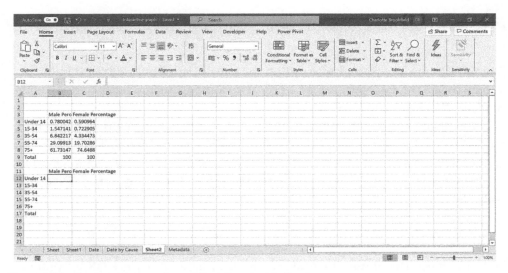

Figure 9.14 Pasting data to make an interactive chart in Excel

In the first, newly empty cell (cell B12 in Figure 9.14), type the following formula: '=IF($A$1=1, B4, NA())'. In this example, the cell B4 is used in the formula as this corresponds to the equivalent cell in the table above, which contains data. The formula tells Excel that when cell A1 has a number '1' inserted, it should present the number of males that died under the age of 14 in 2017. If we also want data on the number of males in the different age brackets to be displayed, we must drag the formula down. Because we have used the $ sign either side of the cell reference A1, there is no need to amend the formula as we drag it down.

At present, all the cells in the second table state '#N/A'. This is because cell A1 is empty. If we enter the number '1' in cell A1, the table will fill with data (see Figure 9.15).

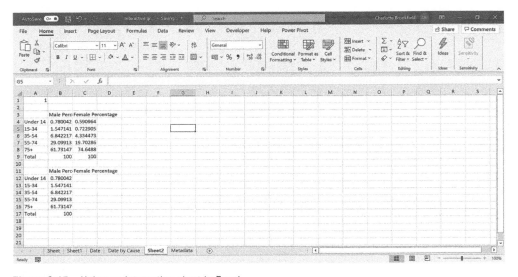

Figure 9.15 Using an interactive chart in Excel

The process now needs to be repeated for the female data. This time the formula will state: '=IF($A$1=2, C4, NA())'. This tells Excel to display the female data only when the number '2' is entered into cell A1 (see Figure 9.16).

Rather than changing the number in cell A1 to dictate what data is visible (male or female), you can create option buttons. In this example, the option buttons and the graph will be on a new worksheet in the Excel Workbook. To insert the option buttons, the Developer tab needs to be visible along the top toolbar. If this is not visible, you will need to go to:

File > Options > Customize Ribbon

and then select '**Developer**' in '**Main Tabs**' (see Figure 9.17). Click **OK** to continue.

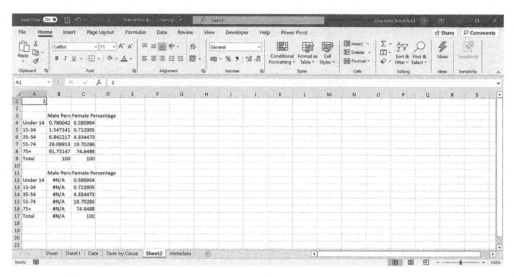

Figure 9.16 Using the interactive chart in Excel to display female data

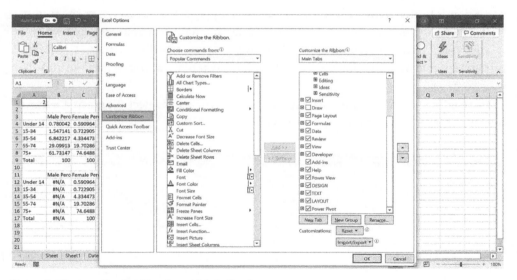

Figure 9.17 Inserting the 'Developer' tab in Excel

Once the Developer tab appears, you are able to insert option buttons. Under '**Developer**', select '**Insert**' and then '**Option Button (Form Controls)**' (see Figure 9.18).

Developer > Insert > Option Button (Form Controls)

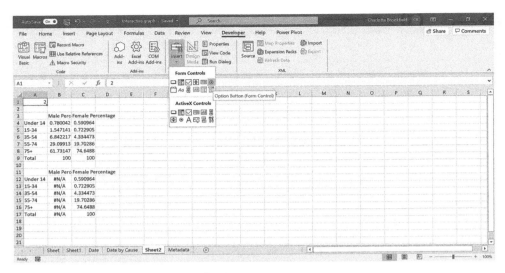

Figure 9.18 Inserting option buttons in Excel

Select where you would like your first option button to appear and give it an appropriate name; in this example, 'Male' is used. It is important that option button 1 corresponds to the column in the data table that appears when you insert the number '1' in cell A1 in your worksheet. In this example, the male data appears when we enter '1' into cell A1 and, therefore, option button 1 must be labelled as male. The process is then repeated as many times as necessary, until you have all the option buttons that you need.

Once all your option buttons are in place, right click and select '**Format Control**' (see Figure 9.19). This will open a new window.

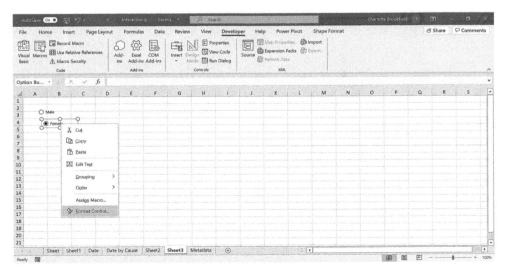

Figure 9.19 Formatting the control of option buttons in Excel

In the new window, select '**Unchecked**' and, for the '**Cell Link**', select the A1 cell which you used in the first part of this task. Click **OK**. You will now notice that when you select the 'Female' option box, the female data appears, and when you select the 'Male' option box, the male data appears.

To create an interactive people graph, highlight the second table of data (the interactive data) and follow the steps presented above. You can then press the option buttons to display either the male or the female data (see Figures 9.20 and 9.21).

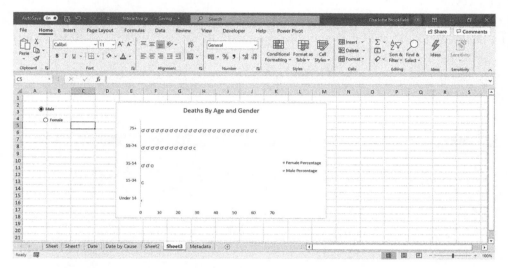

Figure 9.20   An interactive graph in Excel (male data)

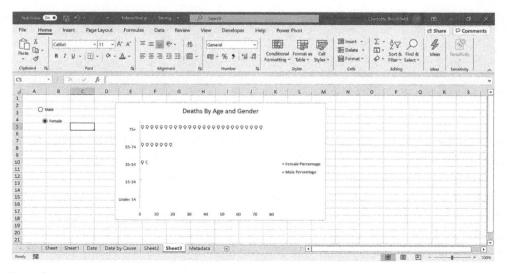

Figure 9.21   An interactive graph in Excel (female data)

Different graph types can be made interactive, so it is worthwhile looking at all the different options available.

9.8.3 Out-of-100-people interactive graphs

Using Excel it is possible to make dynamic, interactive graphs which display the percentage of participants who answered in a particular way to a survey question, in an accessible and visually attractive manner. For example, let's say that I know that 12% of people in my organisation agreed with the statement 'the working day should be made longer', I could make an infographic to display this data, as opposed to just presenting the statistic.

To begin, you need to list the numbers 1–10 repeatedly 10 times (see the example in Figure 9.22).

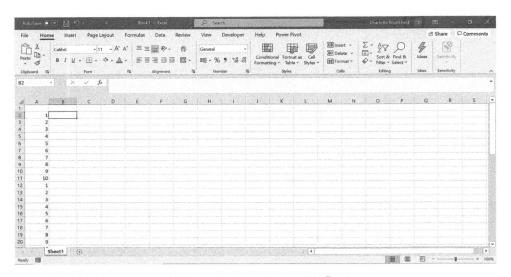

Figure 9.22 Setting up an out-of-100-people interactive graph in Excel

In the adjacent column, enter the number 5 next to the first block of 10, then for the next block enter the number 10, the next 15, and so on, all the way up to 50. It is important that you increase the value in equal size increments for each block of 10 to ensure the spacing is equidistant in the final infographic. Figure 9.23 demonstrates this. The information inserted in these two columns ensures that your resultant infographic contains 10 rows of data with 10 data points each. This means a total of 100 data points will be displayed on your infographic.

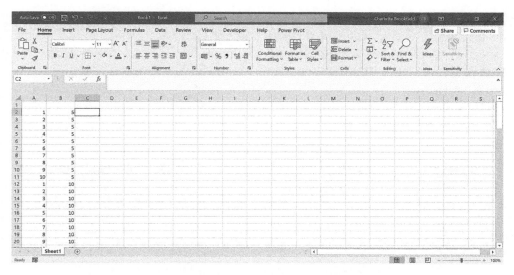

Figure 9.23 Inserting multiples of 5 for an out-of-100-people interactive graph in Excel

Highlight the two columns of data and select the **Insert** tab from the top toolbar. In the '**Charts**' menu, select '**Scatter**'.

Insert > Charts > Scatter

This should create a graph with 100 dots, as seen in Figure 9.24.

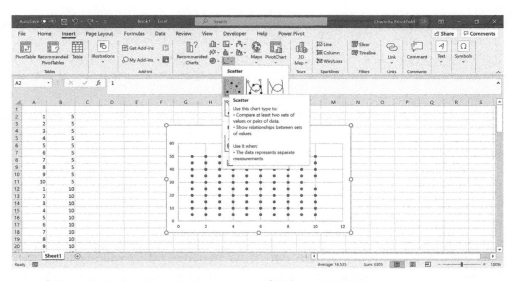

Figure 9.24 Inserting scatter graph to make an out-of-100-people interactive graph

You now need to select an appropriate icon for your infographic. In this example the people icon is used to represent the percentage of participants who agreed with the statement 'the working day should be made longer'. To choose an icon, go to the **Insert** tab and select '**Illustration**'. From this menu, select '**Icons**'. This process is shown in Figure 9.25.

Insert > Illustration > Icons

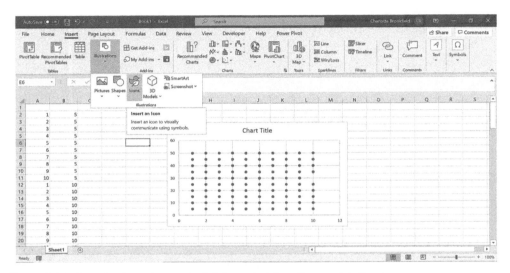

Figure 9.25 Inserting icons in an out-of-100-people interactive graph in Excel

Choose an appropriate icon and click '**Insert**'. Make your icon smaller, remembering that it is going to replace the dots in your scatter graph. Copy and paste your icon and fill one icon with grey and the other with a more vibrant colour such as blue or orange (see Figure 9.26).

Click the grey icon and select '**Copy**' or use the shortcut CTRL+C. Then click a dot on the scatter graph and hold down CTRL+V. This will change all the dots in your scatter graph to your grey icon. If your icons overlap slightly, simply make your graph a little bigger.

The next step is to create a formula so that Excel knows how many icons to shade in your alternative colour, depending on the percentage that you wish to display. To do this, in the column adjacent to the data (in this example column C), enter the formula '=IF(Count(B2:$B$101)<=$C$1,B2, NA())'. Once you have entered this formula, drag it down until you reach cell C101. After this, when you enter different numbers in cell C1, the values in column C on your worksheet will change (see Figure 9.27). Excel will use this information to determine how many icons to shade in the alternative colour.

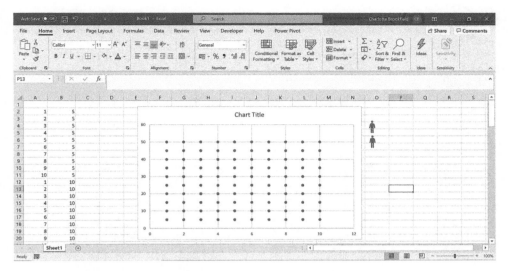

Figure 9.26 Colour coding icons for an out-of-100-people interactive graph in Excel

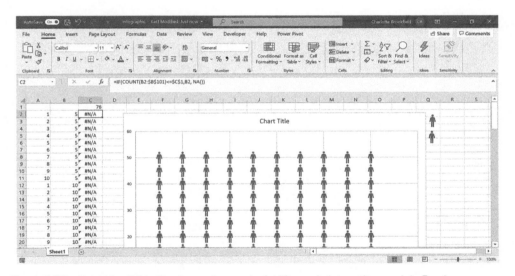

Figure 9.27 Using the IF function to create an out-of-100-people interactive graph in Excel

Make sure that you enter a number into cell C1. In this example, we have inserted 76, meaning that 76% of participants agreed with our statement and that we want to shade 76 icons in our graph in colour. Highlight column C from cell C2 all the way to cell C101. Select copy or use the shortcut CTRL+C and then in the scatter graph select an icon and use the shortcut CTRL+V. Little dots should appear on your icons as seen in Figure 9.28.

Now click your coloured icon to the side of your scatterplot, select copy and then select the icons on the scatter graph and use the shortcut CTRL+V to paste. You will now see that some of your icons are grey and some are coloured. In this example, as cell C1 states, 76 of the icons are in colour and the remaining 24 are in grey (see Figure 9.29).

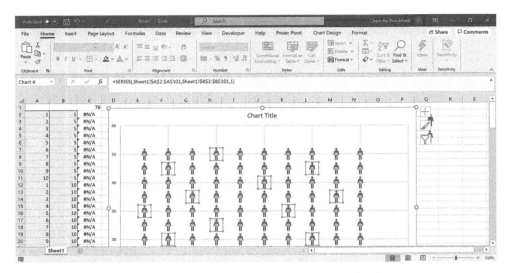

Figure 9.28 Inserting data in an out-of-100-people interactive graph in Excel

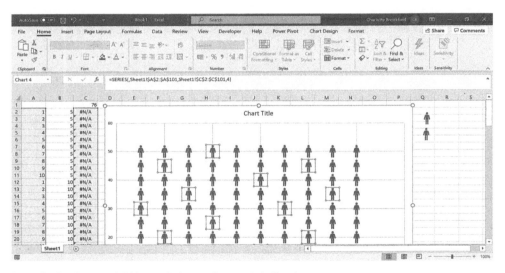

Figure 9.29 An out-of-100-people interactive graph in Excel

However, to complete this infographic you need to reverse the *x*-axis (the horizontal axis) on the scatter graph. This will make the infographic more intuitive and easy to read as the empty/unfilled icons will be on right as opposed to the left. To do this, select the *x*-axis, right click and select the option '**Format Axis**' (see Figure 9.30).

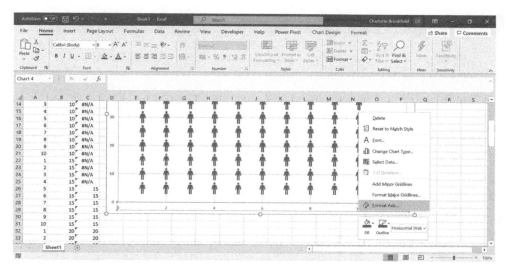

Figure 9.30 Reversing the *x*-axis in an out-of-100-people interactive graph in Excel

Using the menu on the right-hand side, check the option '**Values in reverse order**' (see Figure 9.31).

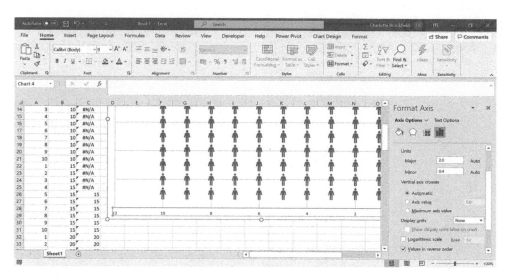

Figure 9.31 Formatting values in reverse order in Excel

To complete the infographic, remove both the vertical and horizontal gridlines. Also, select the axis and delete both separately. This should leave you with the infographic shown in Figure 9.32.

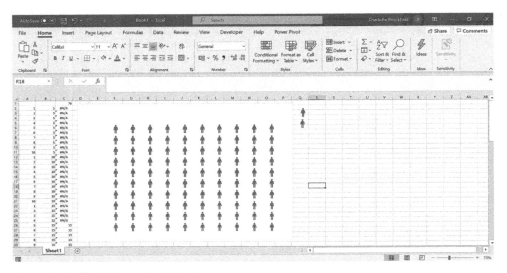

Figure 9.32   Final infographic in Excel

If you change the value in cell C1, the number of icons shaded will also change. This means that it can be helpful to save this template and then use this infographic for multiple projects reporting different statistics as it can be quickly and easily updated. In Figure 9.33, the percentage has been changed to 12.

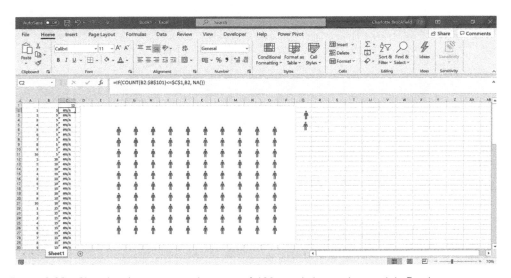

Figure 9.33   Changing the percentage in an out-of-100-people interactive graph in Excel

9.8.4 Maps in Excel

When you have geographical data, it can be advantageous to create filled maps to show this data. Such maps enable your audience to see quickly how your data is distributed over a geographical area. Excel allows you to create maps so that you can compare your data across different geographical regions. The geographical variables that Excel recognises include countries, states, regions, counties, provinces, postcodes or zip codes.

In this example, data from the European Quality of Life Time Series (2007 and 2011) is used to demonstrate how filled maps can be created in Excel. To insert the map, highlight the data and then, under the '**Insert**' tab, select '**Maps**', '**Filled Map**' (see Figure 9.34).

Insert > Maps> Filled Map

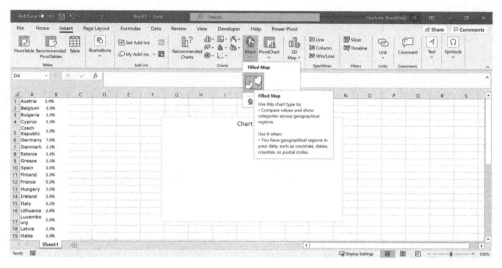

Figure 9.34   Inserting a filled map in Excel

The map will instantly appear. You can then format the map, add a title and change the colours as you wish. Filled maps are easy and quick to make; however, they are not always able to map data accurately. For instance, while the filled map does not have issues mapping some of the local authorities in Wales, others cannot be found. In these instances, you need to use the 3D Maps option.

For the example here, data from StatsWales on the number of rough sleepers (2018/19) has been used. For Excel 2016 onwards, the 3D Maps option is available in the top toolbar automatically. For older versions of Excel, the 3D Maps function is an Add-In option. To insert a 3D map in Excel you must first ensure that your data is formatted as a table. To do this, highlight the data and, under the '**Insert**' tab, select '**Table**' (see the example in Figure 9.35). When the new window opens, if appropriate, select '**My table has headers**' and click **OK**.

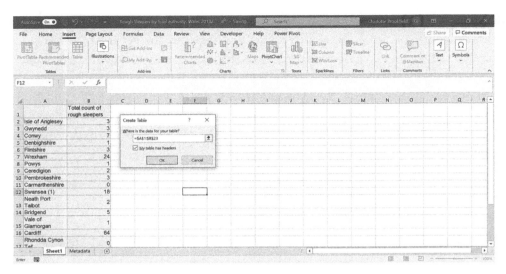

Figure 9.35   Formatting data into a table in Excel

To create a 3D map, begin by highlighting the data that you wish to map. Under '**Insert**', select '**3D Map**' and then choose the option '**Open 3D Maps**' as shown in Figure 9.36.

Insert > 3D Map > Open 3D Maps

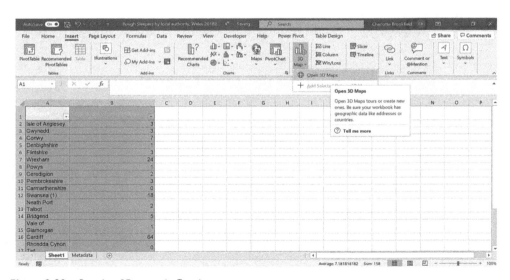

Figure 9.36   Opening 3D maps in Excel

When the 3D map opens, double-check that location data has been properly recognised. In this example, the box shows that the local authority data has been identified as state/province data and therefore is coded correctly (Figure 9.37). However, if this was incorrect, you can use the drop-down menu to change the data type to postcode, city, county, and so on.

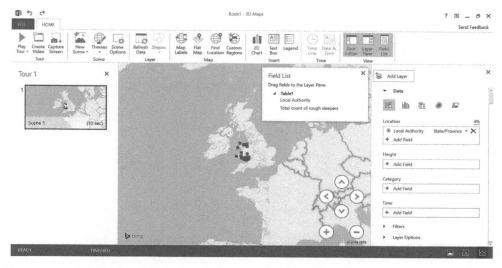

Figure 9.37   Checking location data is correctly coded in Excel

To display effectively the level of homelessness in each local authority, you can use either a column chart or a heat map. With the column chart, Excel will insert a bar to represent each local authority; each bar will be a different height depending on the level of homelessness in each area, whereas, with the heat map option, Excel will shade each authority a different colour depending on the level of homelessness reported in each area.

To insert the column chart, ensure '**Column chart**' is selected in the window on the right-hand side (this is the default option). In the '**Height**' menu, select '**Add Field**' and choose the variable that you wish to map – in this example, '**Total count of rough sleepers**' (see Figure 9.38).

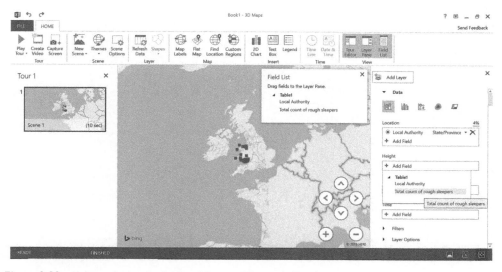

Figure 9.38   Using columns to display data on a 3D map in Excel

This will change the height of the bars, with the taller bars representing the local authorities with the greatest number of reported rough sleepers. It is possible to zoom in and out using the plus and minus signs, this can help you better identify the areas which have high numbers of rough sleepers. In Figure 9.39, it seems that there is a greater prevalence of rough sleepers in the south of the country and particularly so in the south east where the capital city (Cardiff) is located.

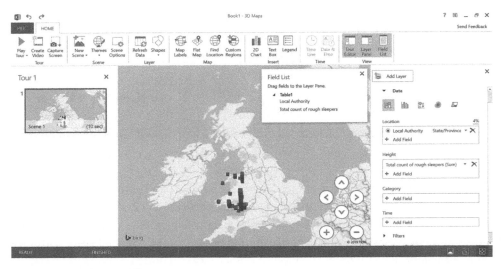

Figure 9.39   A 3D map in Excel

Alternatively, you may wish to present this data using the heat map function. To do this, select heatmap from the menu on the right-hand side (Figure 9.40). This time, under the '**Value**' menu click '**Add Field**' and select the variable of interest.

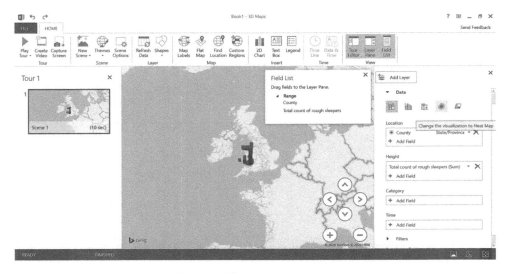

Figure 9.40   Heat map option on 3D maps in Excel

In this example, the areas with higher numbers of rough sleepers appear in a dark colour, while the local authorities with relatively few rough sleepers are shaded more lightly (see Figure 9.41).

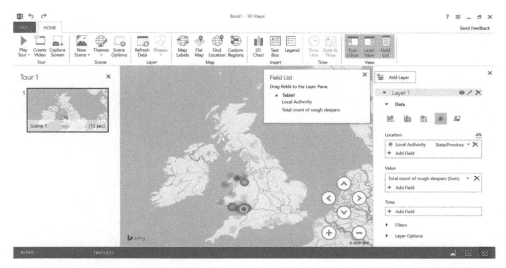

Figure 9.41   A 3D heat map in Excel

Under '**Layer Options**', you can customise your map and change the range and choice of colours used. Once you are happy with your map, select the **Capture Screen** option from the top toolbar. You will then be able to paste your map into a Microsoft Word document or Microsoft PowerPoint presentation.

Research Posters

Look at research posters online. Use Table 9.3 to highlight what features make a good research poster and what features make a bad research poster. Come back to this table when you design your own research poster.

Table 9.3   Features of good and bad research posters

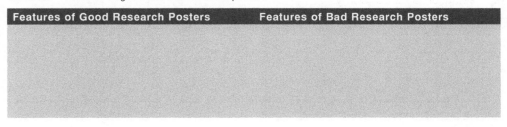

Features of Good Research Posters	Features of Bad Research Posters

(Continued)

Table 9.3 (Continued)

Features of Good Research Posters	Features of Bad Research Posters

Creating an Infographic

Find a statistic that has been in the news this week and create an infographic to represent this statistic. Once you have made your infographic, see whether any of the media coverage surrounding your statistic has made a similar visual representation. Which visual representation is best and why?

....

....

....

....

Further Reading

de Vries, R. 2019. Bad Graphics. In: de Vries, R. *Critical Statistics.* London: Red Globe Press, pp. 156–191.

Evergreen, S.D.H. 2017. *Presenting Data Effectively: Communicating Your Findings for Maximum Impact* (2nd edn). London: Sage.

O'Leary, Z. 2018. *Little Quick Fix: Present Your Research.* London: Sage.

Tufte, E.R. 2001. *The Visual Display of Quantitative Information.* Cheshire, CT: Graphics Press.

Skills Checklist for Chapter 9

Use the checklist provided to track your learning and to highlight areas where you may need to do some additional reading.

	I can do this confidently	I could do this if I had a little more practice	I need more help with this
Create a research poster			
Create a research presentation			
Format tables			
Format charts and graphs			

Ideas for Teachers/Instructors

Collate a number of infographics from various sources (online, newspapers, etc.); you can even ask students to bring in one or two examples of infographics that they have seen. On a wall/board, set up the axes in Figure 9.42 and ask students to place the infographics in the most relevant quadrants. Infographics placed in the top left quadrant will be attractive but not informative. Those in the bottom left quadrant will be the worst – both uninformative and unattractive. Meanwhile, those in the bottom right quadrant will be informative but not particularly attractive. The remaining infographics in the top right quadrant will be both attractive and informative and these are what students should be aiming for in their own work. Ask the students to consider the criteria they used to place the infographics in each quadrant and what features the ones in the top right quadrant share.

(Continued)

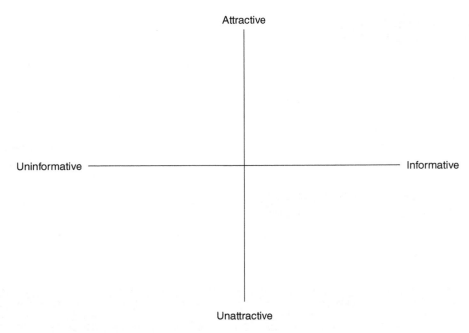

Figure 9.42 Axes for sorting infographics

REFERENCES

Datasets

European Foundation for the Improvement of Living and Working Conditions. (2015). *European Quality of Life Time Series, 2007 and 2011: Open Access*, [data collection], UK Data Service, Accessed 8 April 2020. http://doi.org/10.5255/UKDA-SN-7724-1

Ipsos MORI, Social Research Institute. (2016). *Public Attitudes to Animal Research Survey, 2016*, [data collection], UK Data Service, Accessed 8 April 2020. http://doi.org/10.5255/UKDA-SN-8059-1

NHS England. (2018). *The GP Patient Survey 2018*, [data collection], UK Data Service, Accessed 4 June 2019. http://doi.org/10.5255/UKDA-SN-853308

Office for National Statistics. (2011). *Projections and Trajectory for the Number of Welsh Speakers Aged Three and Over, 2011 to 2050*, [data collection], StatsWales, Accessed 8 April 2020. https://statswales.gov.wales/Catalogue/Welsh-Language

Office for National Statistics, Social Survey Division. (2015). *Opinions and Lifestyle Survey, Well-Being Module, January, February, April and May, 2015*, [data collection], UK Data Service, Accessed 8 April 2020. http://doi.org/10.5255/UKDA-SN-7815-1

Office for National Statistics, University of Manchester. Cathie Marsh Institute for Social Research (CMIST). UK Data Service. (2016). *Living Costs and Food Survey, 2013: Unrestricted Access Teaching Dataset*. [data collection]. 2nd Edition. UK Data Service. http://doi.org/10.5255/UKDA-SN-7932-2.

Office for National Statistics. (2018). *Death Registrations Summary Tables – England and Wales 2017*, [data collection], Office of National Statistics, Accessed 8 April 2020. https://www.ons.gov.uk/peoplepopulationandcommunity/birthsdeathsandmarriages/deaths/datasets/deathregistrationssummarytablesenglandandwalesreferencetables

Office for National Statistics. (2019). *Living Costs and Food Survey, 2013: Unrestricted Access Teaching Dataset*, [data collection], *2nd Edition*, Office for National Statistics, [original data producer(s)], Accessed 8 April 2020. http://doi.org/10.5255/UKDA-SN-7932-2

Office for National Statistics, Social Survey Division. (2019). *Quarterly Labour Force Survey Household Dataset, January–March, 2015*, [data collection], UK Data Service, *4th Edition* Accessed 8 April 2020. http://doi.org/10.5255/UKDA-SN-7816-3

Police Service of Northern Ireland, Statistics Branch. (2016). *Northern Ireland Police Recorded Injury Road Traffic Collision Data, 2015: Open Access*, [data collection], UK Data Service, Accessed 8 April 2020. http://doi.org/10.5255/UKDA-SN-8021-1

Welsh Government. (2020). *Rough Sleepers by Local Authority 2018/19*, [data collection], StatsWales, Accessed 8 April 2020. https://statswales.gov.wales/ Catalogue/Housing/Homelessness/Rough-Sleepers/roughsleepers-by-localauthority

Whiteley, P.F., Saunders, D. (2014). *British Election Study 2010: Campaign Internet Data*, [data collection], UK Data Service, Accessed 4 June 2019. http://doi.org/10.5255/ UKDA-SN-7530-1

Readings

Allison, P.D. 1999. *Multiple Regression: A Primer*. London: Sage.

Barton, E.E. and Reichow, B.R. 2012. Guidelines for Graphing Data with Microsoft Office 2007, Office 2010 and Office for Mac 2008 and 2011. *Journal of Early Intervention* 34(3), pp. 129–150.

Bors, D. 2018. Descriptive Statistics. In: Bors. D. *Data Analysis for Social Sciences: Integrating Theory and Practice*. London: Sage, pp. 22–80.

Burrows, R. and Savage, M. 2014. After the Crisis? Big Data and the Methodological Challenges of Empirical Sociology. *Big Data and Society* 1(1), pp. 1–6.

Carmines, E.G. and Zeller, R.A. 1980. *Quantitative Applications in the Social Sciences: Reliability and Validity Assessment*. London: Sage.

Chamberlain, J., Hillier, J. and Signoretta, P. 2015. Counting Better? An Examination of the Impact of Quantitative Method Teaching on Statistical Anxiety and Confidence. *Active Learning in Higher Education* 16(1), pp. 51–66.

Cohen, R. 2014. Playing with Numbers: Using Top Trumps as an Ice-Breaker and Introduction to Quantitative Methods. *Enhancing Learning in the Social Sciences* 6(2), pp. 21–29.

de Vries, R. 2019. Bad Graphics. In: de Vries, R. *Critical Statistics*. London: Red Globe Press, pp. 156–191.

ESRC. 2019. *Our Core Principles*. Available at: https://esrc.ukri.org/funding/guidance-for-applicants/research-ethics/our-core-principles/ [Accessed 30 July 2019].

Evergreen, S.D.H. 2017. *Presenting Data Effectively. Communicating Your Findings for Maximum Impact* (2nd edn). London: Sage.

Grey, D. 2018. *Doing Research in the Real World* (5th edn). London: Sage.

Haaker, M. 2019. *Little Quick Fix: Choose Your Statistical Test*. London: Sage.

Jones, R.C. 2020. *Essential Maths Skills for Exploring Social Data*. London: Sage.

MacInnes, J. 2018a. *Effective Teaching Practice in Q-Step Centres*. Available at: https:// www.nuffieldfoundation.org/sites/default/files/files/Effective%20teaching%20 practice%20in%20Q-Step%20Centres_FINAL.pdf [Accessed 5 July 2019].

MacInnes, J. 2018b. *Little Quick Fix: Know Your Numbers*. London: Sage.

MacInnes, J. 2019a. *Little Quick Fix: Know Your Variables*. London: Sage.

MacInnes, J. 2019b. *Little Quick Fix: Statistical Significance*. London: Sage.

MacInnes, J. 2019c. *Little Quick Fix: See Numbers in Data*. London: Sage.

Minitab. 2016. *What Are Degrees of Freedom in Statistics?* Available at: https://blog. minitab.com/blog/statistics-and-quality-data-analysis/what-are-degrees-of-freedom-in-statistics#:~:text=Degrees%20of%20freedom%20are%20often,vary%20 when%20estimating%20statistical%20parameters [Accessed 30 July 2019].

Nassif, N. and Khalil, Y. 2006. Making a Pie as a Metaphor for Teaching Scale Validity and Reliability. *American Journal of Evaluation* 27(3), pp. 393–398.

O'Leary, Z. 2018. *Little Quick Fix: Present Your Research*. London: Sage.

Pallant, J. 2007. *SPSS Survival Manual – A Step by Step Guide to Data Analysis Using SPSS for Windows* (3rd edn). Maidenhead: Open University Press.

Ryan, L. and Golden, A. 2006. 'Tick the Box Please': A Reflexive Approach to Doing Quantitative Social Research. *Sociology* 40(6), pp. 1191–2000.

Savage, M. and Burrows, R. 2007. The Coming Crisis of Empirical Sociology. *Sociology* 41(5), pp. 885–899.

Tufte, E.R. 2001. *The Visual Display of Quantitative Information*. Cheshire, CT: Graphics Press.

UK Data Service. *Ten Top Tips for Citing Data*. Available at: https://www.ukdataservice. ac.uk/media/622247/toptentips.pdf [Accessed 30 July 2019].

Warner, B. and Rutledge, J. 1999. Checking the Chips Ahoy! Guarantee. *Chance* 12(1), pp. 10–14.

Warner, C.B. and Meehan, A.M. 2001. Microsoft Excel as a Tool for Teaching Basic Statistics. *Teaching of Psychology* 28(4), pp. 295–298.

Wheelan, C. 2013. Correlation: How Does Netflix Know What Movies I Like? In: Wheelan, C. *Naked Statistics: Stripping the Dread from Data*. London: W.W. Norton, pp. 58–67.

Williams, M., Payne, G., Hodgkinson, L. and Poade, D. 2008. Does British Sociology Count? Sociology Students' Attitudes Toward Quantitative Methods. *Sociology* 42(5), pp. 1003–1021.

INDEX

Note: Figures and tables are indicated by page numbers in bold print. The letter 'b' after a page number stands for bibliographical information in a Further Reading section.